Praise for No Ordinary Time

In No Ordinary Time *and its daily readings for one week, Jan Phillips has packed a lifetime of "AHA's"—thoughts that suddenly give us clarity about our-selves and other selves, the world around us. You will keep sentences in your mind, on your bulletin board, in your pocket and in your heart.*
Gloria Steinem, activist, author of Revolution from Within

Superb book for finding inspiration and guidance for maneuvering through these extraordinary times. Jan Phillips is spot on in knowing what it takes to get us through into the world we all want. Don't hide this book on a shelf but keep it always in sight to go back to again and again. Elisabet Sahtouris, PhD
Evolution biologist and futurist, author of EarthDance: Living Systems in Evolution

The Book of Hours without a Monastery, Psalms without a Psalmody, Prayer without Gregorian Chant! Jan Phillips weaves an intriguing and inspiring tapes-try synthesizing the wisdom embodied in an ancient tradition with the spiritual awakening engaging sojourners of the 21st century. This book provides a cre-ative synthesis from monastery to market-place, from psalm ⸱etry, from *monastic time to the sacredness of every day, and e* ⸱an *Phillips has provided an inspiring resource fo* ⸱hu, au-thor of *Evolutionary Faith*

Jan Phillips is that rare blend of deep, c. ⸱ neart and true *visionary. Her clear and special talent to* ⸱⸱⸱⸱u to inspire action is *needed now more than ever as we all try ⸱* ⸱⸱⸱⸱⸱⸱e these extraordinary times.*
Rev. Wendy Craig-Purcell, Unity Center of San Diego, author of Ask Yourself This

No Ordinary Time *is not so much a book to be read as a sacred moment by moment practice to be engaged in. This is in stark contrast to most books whose ideas we read and forget the next day. If you are committed to exploring and living your destiny in service to life,* No Ordinary Time *is an extraordinarily practical wisdom teaching and gift you can give yourself that can help you em-body the Divine in your own unique way.* Jeff Hutner, editor, *New Paradigm Digest*

An out-of-the-box Book of Hours that will stir your soul, stretch your mind, and embolden your contributions to mending the planet. Jan Phillips blends creativity, mysticism, and spiritual practice into startling and illuminating new configurations.
Frederic and Mary Ann Brussat, authors of Spiritual Literacy

NO ORDINARY TIME
THE RISE OF SPIRITUAL INTELLIGENCE AND EVOLUTIONARY CREATIVITY

A BOOK OF HOURS FOR A PROPHETIC AGE

JAN PHILLIPS

No Ordinary Time —
The Rise of Spiritual Intelligence and Evolutionary Creativity

A Book of Hours for a Prophetic Age

First Edition
ISBN 0-9774213-4-1

Published by Livingkindness Foundation
5187 Arlene Place
San Diego, CA 92117

www.livingkindnessfoundation.org
www.janphillips.com

Printed and bound in the United States of America

Cover design by Thomas Gaebel
Interior design and illustrations by Thomas Gaebel
Cover photo from NASA, taken by Hubble Space Telescope

Acknowledgements

I give thanks to the Source of Life Itself, to the Cosmos, and to the Great Mystery that unfolds every second of the day.

To my Mom, who at 88 years, stretches my mind and brings me joy every moment I'm with her.

To my dear friends Rande Wegman, Penelope Bourk and Ruth Westreich who feed me in innumerable ways and keep me balanced and buoyant.

To my Gnostic Gospel Choir who co-created the *Singing for the Soul* CD and inspired many of the songs in this book.

To Annie O'Flaherty who painstakingly edited this book to spare you my excesses.

To Diarmuid O'Murchu whose work has inspired me for years and who took the time to read this manuscript before it went to print.

To Tommy Gaebel, my cousin and cohort in all things creative, for his genius in designing this beautiful cover and book.

To my Evolutionary Creativity group at Unity Center for demonstrating what evolutionary creativity looks and sounds like in real life.

To the International Women's Writing Guild who invited me to teach at their summer conference twenty years ago and changed the course of my life.

To all the people who've attended my workshops in the US, Canada, Nigeria, and Ireland who opened your lives like a book and gave me access to your deepest wisdom.

And to all the artists, poets, writers and musicians who have had the courage to put your work out there so it could find me and move me forward on the path.

CONTENTS

INTRODUCTION

Seven times a day do I praise thee. Psalm 119:164

These are no ordinary times. We are witnessing and participating in an evolutionary leap unlike anything in our history. There is evidence in the human family of an upward shift in consciousness, a maturing spirituality, a connectedness that grows more intimate and global by the day. And that uplift is countered by the dissolution of myths that no longer serve us and the demise of institutions that have underpinned our culture since the beginning of our history. Our planetary worldview is shifting to wide angle as we awaken to the reality of our interdependence.

We are the myth-makers and co-creators of the 21st century, the prophets and writers of new sacred texts. Growing up spiritually is a requirement of us this hour. There is no Geppetto God out there pulling strings. We are the vessels of the   Divine, agents of Supreme Intelligence, neural cells of our home planet, and it is our job now to call God home, to tend to the kingdom that is all around us, and to create stories and cultures of hope and compassion.

This book is a call to mindfulness, a reminder that evolutionary action begins with stillness, that visionary ideas arise from spiritual practice. It is a book for people conscious of their power and ready to co-create new sacraments and ceremonies that celebrate the Divine dwelling within us. It is a handbook for people committed to justice, peacemaking and spiritual integrity who are eager to evolve themselves spiritually and creatively.

While its form is taken from the medieval *Book of Hours*, its content stretches into the future—an ancient chalice for tomorrow's wine. It is a guide to reclaiming your spiritual authority, rethinking your inherited beliefs so you can create a life that is prophetic, ecstatic and true to your soul. It bridges the One and the many, East and West, masculine and feminine, darkness and light through an array of stories, poems, prayers and songs.

The *Book of Hours* originated in the Middle Ages as a way for people to stay spiritually mindful. The Jewish practice of saying prayers during the day was adopted by Christians as the basis for their daily spiritual practice. The Jews of the pre-Christian era had a source of devotional verse in the Book of Psalms, which included 150 prayers, poems and hymns. Christians adopted this book for their own use, and the "Psalter" soon became their main devotional text as well. Monks and nuns recited the Psalms according to guidelines laid out in monastic rules established primarily by St. Benedict.

In order to distinguish the divisions of time between the prescribed prayers, the Catholic Church established the canonical hours, also referred to as the Divine Office. Life in many medieval communities revolved around these hours of the day which were designated as Matins (midnight), Lauds (sunrise), Prime (6:00 a.m.), Terce (9:00 a.m.), Sext (noon), None (3:00 pm), Vespers (sunset), and Compline (9:00 p.m.)

Over the centuries, a number of supplementary texts were added to the Psalter. It became customary, for example, to frame the Psalms with "antiphons"—brief passages that helped to create Christian significance in the old Jewish texts. The antiphons were joined by a variety of prayers, canticles, hymns, readings from the Bible, and dialogues. The book that was developed for lay people who wished to incorporate elements of monasticism into their devotional life was called *The Book of Hours*.

This *Book of Hours* is designed for the same purpose—to give people a way to stay spiritually grounded throughout the day. It is based on the premise that we are in consort with our own Source and Creator, the Invisible One known as God and the visible one known as Earth. I am writing it for the ones who already know there is no distance between the Divine and the mortal, who already engage in an unmediated love affair with the Creator, and who, in such large numbers, have had to leave the churches that refuse to be relevant in these times of crisis. Many of these words will seem blasphemous to religious adherents who think there is only one way to be faithful, but one of the greatest ways we can serve each other is to challenge each other's thoughts.

When the German philosopher Jean Gebser wrote about his vision of the emergence of human consciousness, he referred to the myth of Athena, the Goddess of Wisdom, who was born from the head of Zeus. In *The Ever-Present Origin* (1949) Gebser uses the ancient myth to capture the epic struggle and effort of human development:

> And it would be well for us to be mindful of one actuality: although the wound in the head of Zeus healed, it was once a wound. Every "novel" thought will tear open wounds . . . everyone who is intent upon surviving—not only earth but also life—with worth and dignity, and living rather than passively accepting life, must sooner or later pass through the agonies of emergent consciousness.

If this book does what I hope it does, you may experience some of these agonies as you release the old for what is emerging. I have stretched in my spiritual practice to think and pray not only as a Christian, but as a Jew, a Muslim, a Hindu, a Buddhist, a Native American, an atheist, a post-theist. I try on different hats as I light my candle, and while my thoughts might change or my prayers change, the Presence I am steeped in never alters, the Ground of my Being never moves. No matter what my spiritual stance, awe and adoration are the common ground. As I wrote one day during my morning prayers: "If there is a God, I am in awe. If there is not a God, I am in greater awe."

We are not here to debate what God means. We are here to live out the meaning of God, to BE the God we want to see in the world. This book is a holy book, full of reverence, praise, lamentations, and songs. It is one poet praying, to forces visible and invisible. It is one person sharing her intimacy with the Beloved. It is an adventure in aliveness, a sojourn for the soul. Come along. Let go and lift up.

No Ordinary Time

CHAPTER ONE MONDAY

When I was a child, I spoke and thought and reasoned as a child. But when I grew up, I put away childish things. 1 Corinthians 13:11

AWAKENING

At an early age, I learned that God was a Being who dwelled in a place far from where I ever stood. I learned to commune with the transcendent God of the Above, not the immanent Divine Within. But over the years, as I let go of childish thinking and took responsibility for my spiritual life, my perception of God changed dramatically. I am guided now not so much by teachings that were handed down to me, but by ideas that have risen up from within—a shift that began thirty years ago when I was a young postulant nun in a religious order taking my first theology class.

The Jesuit priest stood in front of the room and asked us what we believed about God. One postulant raised her hand, stood up and said "God made me to show His goodness and to share his everlasting life with me in heaven." I nodded my head in agreement, having memorized this years ago just like everyone else in the room.

The priest looked dismayed. "That's it?" he asked.

"Yes, Father."

"Sit down," he barked, looking around for the next hand.

Up it went, and the next brave soul stood up saying, "In God there are three Divine Persons, really distinct, and equal in all things-the Father, the Son, and the Holy Ghost."

I nodded again, and the priest frowned. "Is that the best you can do?"

"Yes, Father."

"Next," he yelled, as she took her seat, looking around in wonder.

By now, we're all confused, but one more raised her hand.

"God can do all things, and nothing is hard or impossible to Him."

"Sit down," he said.

He rolled his eyes, crossed his arms and surveyed the whole group of us with a kind of silent disdain. By now, I'm feeling anxious and blood is rushing up my neck. I feel hot and sweaty. My first anxiety attack.

"How could he do this?" It seemed so mean. He asked for our ideas about God and yet, when we said them, it felt like he took a sledge hammer and smashed our beliefs into a thousand pieces. A tear rolled down my cheek.

It was a moment of devastating loss, incomprehensible sadness. I felt as if everything I believed in, everything on which I had based my life, was now being challenged. We sat there, thirty of us, for what seemed an eternity, reckoning with the obliteration of God as we had known Him. What if everything we believed wasn't true? Did Father Grabys know something we didn't know?

Finally the priest spoke. "You should be ashamed for having nothing more than catechism answers to this question. Are you just a bunch of parrots, repeating everything you've been taught? Hasn't anyone here gone beyond the Baltimore Catechism in your thinking?"

The air was thick with silence. Hands were folded, eyes cast down. Tears cascaded down my face. I prayed he wouldn't call on me.

"You must come to know what is true about God from your own experience," said the priest. "If you are to be a nun worth your salt, you have to arrive at a faith that is deeper than your learning, one that is rooted in your ultimate concerns and rises up from the nature of who you are."

I looked up at him, wondering how in the world to build a faith from my human nature. Wasn't faith something I was born into? Something I inherited, from the outside? I was a Catholic by default. They told me everything I was supposed to believe. That was the point, wasn't it? I was just lucky to be born into the one true faith. I certainly didn't have anything to *say* about it. That's what infallible popes were for.

I raised my hand and asked him how someone could create a faith from the inside out, and why we even needed to since we knew what we needed to know from the catechism.

"What you believe, that is religion," he said. "Who you are, what you live for—that is faith. And that is what we are here to explore, to create and to declare—our faith and spirituality. You can let go of your beliefs for awhile as you learn how to create a faith that will see you through everything."

I didn't want to let go of any beliefs. They were all I had. And they were enough. I didn't need anything more, or so I thought. As we continued on in the class, the biblical paradox that says we must lose our lives in order to find them suddenly began to make sense. Taking responsibility for our own spirituality was a painstaking process that lasted the entire semester as we worked to find and define our own commitments and ultimate concerns—a task that was supremely challenging for young women who had been taught all their lives *what* to think, but not *how* to think.

We never looked at another catechism, never recited another memorized belief, but step by step, we built a new spirituality for ourselves that was deeply personal and rooted in our ultimate concerns. And every day, during meditation, there was something new and profoundly elegant to contemplate: myself as the creator of my own spiritual path.

The prayers, poems, hymns and reflections that follow are invitations to pause during the day to stay attuned to the Creative Energy coursing through us. They are modern day parables, written for the mystics and prophets of *these* times. They are revelations of a kind, distilled from hours of prayer and silence, and years of noisy living, calling attention to the hungers of the world and our role as co-creators to respond with love.

MATINS (MIDNIGHT)

When I open my eyes, there I find you
When I speak, does your love flow out
When I touch one in pain, do you heal them
When I am silent do you bathe me in joy.

Carl Jung wrote that "One does not become enlightened by imagining figures of light, but by making the darkness conscious." But what training do we have for this? How do we enter into our own depths and make sense of the dark and penetrating mysteries? How do we awaken to our own knowing? How do we remember what we came here for, so the grand mission of our soul can be the propelling force of our lives?

How has it happened that, after all these years, we are still seeking, still dissatisfied, still comparing ourselves to this one and that, always coming up short? It is because we have listened to the voices outside of us and not to the sound of our own soul. We absorb the absurdities of this culture and shape our thoughts to its contours, rather than thinking originally and creating a jubilantly authentic life. This is a total abdication of our original bliss.

Our soul took on a body to do its work in this earthly milieu, and now most of us have forgotten the mission we came for. How many are trapped in meaningless, maddening jobs just to support a life we never came here to live? And it happens almost by default. Almost overnight. We have a notion, when we're young, of a life that is fitting, in tune with our spirit. We start in that direction, but the cultural undertow takes us down. Everyone talks about money and new cars and big houses. No one says anything about work that matters. No one mentions the soul, the spirit, the passion and energy that comes from giving ourselves to something we love. Joy gets connected to *having,* and *being* takes the back seat.

Next thing we know, we're forty, fifty, sixty, and it's taking all our energy to keep what we have. Who ARE we then? What are we doing and why? Where are our choices coming from? Do we even remember our soul's purpose, our heart's desire?

Making the darkness conscious is about removing our blinders, restoring our sight. It is a journey to the deeper voice, past our programming and conditioning, beyond our self-doubts and insecurities. It costs nothing and gives us everything. But we must be prepared for a shattering of what we once held to be true. We survived the dissolution of Santa Claus and the Easter Bunny and we can survive the dissolution of other myths that keep us childish and no longer serve us.

Anthony de Mello, a Jesuit retreat director and psychologist, often said, "It's not that we fear the unknown. You cannot fear something you do not know. It's loss of the known that we fear." And awakening is just that—it's giving up old thoughts and habits that no longer serve us. It's creating our own creeds to live by. It's remembering that we are born creators and that our ultimate, unique creation is our own life.

It's a bit embarrassing, when we first wake up, to realize how much of who we think we are and what we think is real depends on what other people have told us. We are full of inherited voices, most of which were handed down by insecure people trying to pass on what someone told them.

When I was young, I'd ask my mother why my father said terrible things about some groups of people. She'd say to me, "Oh, honey, it's not his fault. It's just what he learned." And I'd go away confused every time, wondering if he was a grown-up, why didn't he think his *own* thoughts? Why did he have to keep thinking what people *told* him to think?

Anyone who has been shaped in any way by religious traditions has been exposed to a tremendous amount of contradictions. Sacred texts have been mistranslated, misinterpreted, and misunderstood for millennia. Depending on our programming, we can find in them anything we need to support our bad behaviors—sexism, racism, homophobia, slavery, violence.

That is why we need to inquire within, dip down into our own well of wisdom and come up with a faith that is true to who we are and what we know. If something you've been taught doesn't ring true, alter it. If it's too small to contain your magnitude, expand it. If it polarizes people, excludes people, leads to anything other than understanding and openness, broaden it or abandon it. It is up to us to create new canons of compassion and morality. We cannot wait for leaders to rise up from the masses and save us from ourselves—we are the leaders and this is our time.

Great Being of light and darkness,
I stand with you and in you
a citizen of earth
a co-creator of culture.

9

I am the bulb to your Light
and your radiance illumines the paths I take.
Only praises ring out from my lips,
tears of joy flow like rivers down my cheeks.

This is the beginning of a new day. Each day you awaken to a canvas of twenty-four hours, ready for what only YOU can create. What will you make of this gift you've been given? What do you need to fulfill your mission?

LAUDS (SUNRISE)

Though they speak of the distance between us
Though they think you are light-years away
I've awakened to find you within me
As I breathe, you walk through my door.

I light my morning candle
as a humble hello
to You, Invisible One.
It is me here, I say,
from the land of matter.
Word made flesh, I announce
breathing you
(even when I doubt you)
in and out,
in and out.

I am steeped in the mystery
of holy communion
of known and unknown
energy and mass
heaven and earth

If there is a God, I am in awe.
If there is not a God,

I am in greater awe.

I bow like a spelunker
in the cave of mystery.
I pray from this cave
I cut all ties to certainty
I rejoice in wonder,
bend my knee to the darkness

Inside me there is a spark
called my spirit
I spend my days calling out
thanks for this
in every direction,
to the right and the left,
the above and below,
and I will do this faithfully
till my last breath
vanishes one day
into the blue sky of You.

Your own Self-Realization is the greatest service you can render the world.
Ramana Maharshi

Self-realization, or spiritual awakening, is the actualization of our own divinity. It is a recognition of ourselves in all things and all things in ourselves, found through the contemplation of things as they are. The opposite of selfishness, it is a manifestation of ourselves as gift and mirror to others. The deeper one's self-awareness, the clearer we can reflect the other.

Self-realization is an exploration into the complexities and contradictions of life, an attempt to plumb the opposites until we arrive finally at the Oneness that contains them. It is a process of observation, an astute probing into reality, past our learned illusions of separateness into the exuberant experience of our connectedness.

When we observe something deeply, we enter into it, become one with it. Something of its essence enters into us, and we are changed in the process.

When we read a novel, see a play, listen to a story, we enter into its world, place ourselves in the scene and experience the drama and conflicts as if they were ours. We often come away from someone else's creation with a deeper understanding of our own story.

In my quest for the Infinite, I have come to believe that God, Truth, Beauty, Love—all those concepts I associate with the Divine—are not things that are "found" at the end of the path, like the pot of gold at the end of the rainbow, but are rather what I experience on the journey as I travel through life—or perhaps, more explicitly, they are the journey itself.

God, to me, is the universe unfolding, the power and potential within all our lives, the Oak within our acorn selves. We are not separate at all, but intermingled like salt and the sea. The Divine is ever-present in the faces, the scenes, the feelings that pass through my life day to day.

Whenever I'm tempted to speak of God, the words of Lao Tzu come to mind: "He who knows does not speak. He who speaks does not know." Or the Zen saying, "Open mouth, already big mistake." Or St. Augustine, "If you have understood, it is not God." God, like love, is better defined by what it isn't than by what it is. Meister Eckhart, the Christian mystic, wrote that the ultimate leavetaking is the leaving of God for GOD—the final letting go of the limited concept for an experience of the real thing.

When I was young, I prayed to be a martyr. I wanted to show God and everyone else that I loved Him enough to die for him. I wanted to go into battle for Him, be another Joan of Arc, a hero for God's sake.

Now all that's changed. I wouldn't think of dying for God, but am doing my best to live for God—not God as person, but God as Goodness, Justice, Mercy. There are no more lines of separation, only strands of connectedness. My eyes find holiness everywhere, in every living thing, person, in every act of kindness, act of nature, act of grace. Everywhere I look, there God is, looking back.

I have felt the swaying of the elephant's shoulders and now you want me to climb on a jackass? Try to be serious. Mirabai, Hindu mystic poetess and singer (1498-1546)

Dear Invisible One,
I may be all alone out here
but it works better
for me to think not.

Somehow
it's less lonely,
more fun to imagine
an invisible force
shoring up everything I do
from the other side.
Like a wave to my particle self,
hydrogen to my oxygen,
a puzzle that needs my piece
to be complete.

It's moot in the long run—
it is what it is—
and on this plane
will only be that
till I climb the next rung
of awareness
where all heaven breaks loose
Or not.

When it's time to go around the circle and name our commitments, one
woman in the group says, "I'm committed to living in bliss twenty-four hours a
day." A huge roar of laughter follows.
    "You can't really mean it!"
    "You know that's not possible, right?"
    "Great joke! Now what are you *really* committed to?"
    I find myself in one of those pregnant moments. I laugh, at first, but the laugh
turns into a wonder...hmmm, I think, why not?
    Bliss is just a matter of waking up. It means living in the present moment and

not veering off into the past or future. Bliss is what happens when we stop resisting, stop struggling against the events of our lives and start mining them for the jewels they offer. It is the result of choosing the moment instead of clashing with it. Bliss is what bluebirds have, what howling wolves and singing whales have. By itself, without analysis and additions, life is glorious. Perfect. The only thing that keeps us from bliss is our opinion that we don't have it, can't acquire it or hold on to it. When we start to focus on having it, instead of being in it, we become like fish swimming in circles, searching for water.

When his son was born, my brother gave my mother a license plate holder that read, "Happiness is being Chad's grandmother." It survived many winters in upstate New York, but eventually rusted out from the salt they use to melt the ice on wintery roads. Now only half of it remains, but the message is true. It reads: *Happiness is.* Knowing this is the first step in awakening. When happiness *isn't*, it's simply a warning sign that we have nodded off, forgotten the real and added some illusion or expectation to the situation.

Waking up is not easy, but it is the only way to go if we want to live a life with any passion and punch. It means we have to give up blaming. Give up making others responsible for our happiness. Abandon that habit of judging people, dwelling in the negative. Waking up means being able to observe our life as if it were happening to someone else. It means thinking and speaking consciously, knowing that what we think and say on Tuesday becomes the life we live on Thursday. Waking up means we don't see the other as better or less than ourselves. We see the other *as* our self.

PRIME (6:00 AM)

Though others may judge and degrade me,
cast me out for blaspheming your name
Still I will say that I hold you
like a flower in the palm of my heart.

My chiropractor's office was filled with worker's comp cases today. "I don't understand why they're doing this to themselves," he confided to me. "They're overworking, over-stressing, taxing themselves beyond reason. It's like they're on some treadmill and don't know how to get off. They're waiting for someone else to say 'slow down,' but corporate America is never going to say that to their workers. We have to start saying it to ourselves."

In *The Revolt of the Masses*, Jose Ortega y Gasset wrote, "Our life is at all times and before anything else the consciousness of what we can do." Waking up is about clarifying what we can do and what we *cannot* do. If we're aiming for balance, we cannot be checking email, engaging in a conference call, and sorting through papers on our desk all at the same time. Multi-tasking is something we all *can* do, but the question is *should* we? Are we really more efficient when we do several things at once or does it fragment our thinking, fracture our integrity? What does it feel like to you when you are trying to talk with someone who is typing away on a computer or texting as you talk?

An Algonquin elder, when asked the key to happiness responded: "The key to happiness is giving each task all the time it requires." Imagine signs posted at the water cooler, above every desk and workbench, in rest rooms and restaurants: GIVE EACH TASK ALL THE TIME IT REQUIRES.

These days, that seems counter-cultural. To give each task all the time it requires frees us to bring our complete beings to the table—not just our time, but the wisdom we have gathered, the imagination we have access to, the resources of our spirit, our joyfulness, our sense of connection to others. That wholeness is what translates into excellence. That whole-brain, whole-body approach is what leads to extraordinary creativity, breakthrough thinking.

If we are trying to do three things at once, each thing gets only a fraction of our mind, a small chunk of our magnitude. Our contribution then is stunted, stymied by the clutter of other objectives in the way. But if we take one thing at a time and give it our full attention, then each thing we handle gets all of us.

And the same is true for our journey into awareness. It will take time and conscious attention to detail. It will call for practice, discipline, and compassion for yourself as you learn to navigate this new terrain. You will stumble over and over, and every time you notice a faltering, that noticing is a success. Every time you become aware of your thinking and reconfigure it, that is a step ahead. Every conscious re-entry into the present after a foray into the past or future, that, too, is a stride forward.

If you pay attention, you cannot fail. "All the way to heaven *is* heaven," said Catherine of Siena. You have already arrived. The journey is simply to live in that awareness.

Every encounter we have is colored by our thoughts. If we approach an experience with fear or negativity, the experience will be a receptacle for that. If we enter into it with kindness and a sense of communion, the experience will contain that. Our thoughts precede and create our reality. Begin to observe your thoughts and direct them.

Whoever knows the All but fails to know himself lacks everything.
Gospel according to Thomas

Jesus said, "You are the light of the world." Buddha, on his deathbed, said "Be lamps unto yourselves." The Koran says, "Wheresoever you turn, there is the face of God." Light within, light coming through us, light in the presence of all that is. The Masters have said it, but does it ring true? Do these voices resonate with your own knowing? Is it true for you?

If you were asked to think of a person who's of the light, who comes to mind? Why? Is it because there's some purity of intention there? Some steadfastness in commitment? Some sense of inner authority, authenticity, joyfulness? How are you being a light to others? How does the light come through you? How do you experience the light coming through others?

When I think of people I know who are lights in the world, I think of my friends who are fun-loving, imaginative, in love with the lives they are creating day by day. They are the ones who laugh a lot, sing a lot, cry freely, hug tenderly. They talk about themselves, not others. They are spellbound at life's mysteries. They are the ones with more questions than answers. If they are striving for anything, it is to be free of illusion, one with What Is. Their actions are connected to their values. They *are* their thoughts, their words, their feelings. They are the embodiment of the light they believe themselves to be.

How have you learned to be compassionate with yourself so you can better love others? What new things are you discovering about who you are and why you do things?

Imagine the Divine as the Source of Light shining through the prism of earth's atmosphere, breaking into billions of tiny, colorful, radiant refractions called human beings. Imagine that you are that same Light, at a different density. It is only our illusions that shroud the light. Any thought that we are separate from

16

the others, separate from the Source, is all illusion, and any creed that fosters this notion deserves to be forsaken.

The poet Kabir wrote, "If you have not lived through something, it is not true." Experience is an essential part of knowledge. So the question is, "Do I experience myself as a light in this world? Do I operate from this premise? When I set sail in the morning for a day at sea, is this the wind that propels me?" If it is, then how is it obvious to those around me?

TERCE (9:00 A.M.)

In the silence of dawn do I find you
In the roar of the crowd you are there
In the eyes of the foe can I see you
In my enemy's heart do you dwell.

When I first began my spiritual practice in 1989, I committed to 20 minutes of silence in the morning before I got up. I sat in my bed with a candle burning in front of me and a cup of coffee in my hands. I imagined myself as a satellite dish, receiving messages from Mind-at-Large. This poem is the first poem that came through, which turned out to be a song. It's called *Rebecca's Song* because when I inquired into the voice and asked if it had a name, it seemed to say Rebecca. I think the angel she is referring to is the Immanent Divine, the Holy One within.

Rebecca's Song

Now is the time to be mindful of light
to keep the flame going, to give up the fight
for life is a pleasure, it's not meant for pain
let go of the struggle and dance once again

For you all have an angel who sits at your side,
who waits for your calling, who hears every cry
she's there at your service, there as your guide,
so call her, she's waiting with arms open wide.

The God that you're seeking needs not to be sought
you're already one like the sea and the salt
the Source is within you, the force is at hand
it's been in your soul since your life began.

So rejoice, my child, in the gifts that you have
the light of the world is the torch in your hand
and when you get beyond your fear and your pain,
you'll see God in the being who goes by your name.

We can't afford *not* to be thinking now, when it's our very thoughts that are shaping the world. We're facing crises the world has never known, and we're in labor now, trying to birth a new consciousness, evolve a higher form of humanity that comprehends its sacred essence. If we, as a human race, are to make the shift from puberty to full maturity, we must respond to the crisis of our times as every cell in the body responds to a gunshot wound—with unremitting alertness, undivided attention, generous and humble in its service to the whole.

The future ahead of us is the future we create everyday, in our workplaces, our families, our encounters with strangers and friends. Our real work is to imagine the life we want to be living and draw it toward us. It is not to look behind us to see how they did it before, not to rustle through old texts for solutions, but to re-examine everything we've been taught and dismiss whatever divides us from one another.

If you want to wake up, examine the thoughts in your own mind and weigh them against what you know to be true from your own experience. We are the eyes and the ears and the voice of the earth, cells in the body of God collaborating in the continuing creation of our planet. We have one lifetime under this name to speak our truths, to manifest in the world the supreme force of love that cannot be made explicit without our hands, our eyes, our voices and actions.

We are here to make the Invisible visible. No matter what our business cards say, no matter what we are paid to do, no matter how we define ourselves, the essence of our work is spiritual—and it is that element that gives it meaning and magic. When we wake up and take our souls to work, consciously, everything about the workday changes. It becomes a playing field, an opportunity to create what wouldn't exist without us, to see ourselves reflected in others, and mirror them back to themselves. It is a chance to practice being in the moment, choose what is before us. It is an eight hour class in the possibility of bliss.

Every day we experience dozens of encounters. We hear people say things. We notice the behaviors of people. We see and hear ourselves talking and acting. We're in the school of life all day long, but what do we make of it? What do we say at the dinner table when they ask, "What did you learn today?"

I'll tell it to you again
we are flowers in the same garden
descendents of one Mother
you, a rose,
me, an iris
she, a gardenia splashing scent with every breeze

I could go on and on about our likeness
every one of us a leaf on the same tree
a snowflake in the same blizzard
bubbles in the same champagne
can you stop laughing long enough
to digest this mystery?

If these were the headlines of your daily paper
would you eyes pop open with joy?

Do you see the wonder here?
Can you find your adorable face in this house of mirrors?

Do you hear it clearly?
That what you are enveloped in is the body of God
what you were born from is the mother of Life
the air you breathe is their giant exhalation
their sigh of delight after a long night of love

Do you really want to know you're a child of desire
born from the embrace of heaven and earth?
can you bear it? can you be this huge?
embody this mystery?

In case it comes as a bit of a surprise
I'll tell it to you again:
You, my dear, are a beautiful rose
and I am an iris
and all those around us:
flowers in the same garden
descendents of the same Mother

This is the Eden of your beginning and end
This is the Heaven you have sought all along.

Meet this day with clarity and be a light in the darkness. Unfold your arms and let others in. Listen and speak like your life depended on every utterance. Practice truthfulness. Say things about yourself and others in a kindly way. Direct conversations in an upward spiral. Do not collude in negativity. Finding calm in this storm is a matter of mindfulness. We can be at peace every moment if we meet it with awareness and remember our source. The moment we choose peace, it is ours.

SEXT (NOON)

Though the newspapers dwell on disaster
Though the media spreads only fear
I am a beacon of hopefulness
Only light shall I cast on the world.

It is so easy for us to get tangled up in others, to forget what we once knew. How do we keep our knowing fresh if no one ever asks us about it? And why would anyone ask us if we never ask anyone else what they know or really care about? If someone doesn't go first, how do authentic conversations ever get started?

I learned a lesson about going first on a cross country trip a few years ago. My plan was to interview people in small towns about their values, getting the latest scoop on Americans' changing attitudes and spiritual outlook. I'd driven through six states before finally stopping at a restaurant in rural Virginia where I found a young man willing to talk with me.

"I'm trying to get a sense of changing values in this country," I blathered as I rifled through my bag looking for my pad of questions. Finding it, I launched quickly into the first question. "Where did you get your values from?"

"W-H-U-T??" he asked, his brow scrunched up like a furrowed field. I could see he had no idea what I was talking about. Then I heard a little voice in my head. "Go first," it said.

"Oh yeah," I started, "like with me, how I got one of my values was from my Mom who always said, 'If you pass by someone on the street, be sure to look them in the eye and give them a big smile, because they might be having a real bad day and your smile can make all the difference in the world." I told him I never particularly liked that assignment, but I took it on, trusting in my mom's wisdom, and now I can't help but do it. "I've been smiling at people on the street for the last forty years," I told him. "That's a value I got from my Mom."

He sat there silent, his arms folded tight across his chest. Squinting at me, he nodded his head without saying a word. His toothpick shifted from one corner of his mouth to the other while his mind worked the idea like a plow in a pasture.

Finally, the pieces came together. "Ya' mean like when my daddy used to get into his whiskey and whup my butt-and I'd go out on the back porch where my grand-daddy would be rockin' in his chair. He'd see me there, trying not to cry, then he'd say to me, 'Son, I see ya' got some big feelings there. Why don't ya' sit on down under that oak tree and write yourself a poem? That'll help you get them feelings out.' And now I do that, I write poems."

"My grand-daddy always said 'If God has given you a gift that you can give back to people, don't you ever turn your back on it. Whenever you feel a poem coming on, you sit down and write it. And after you write it, find some way to share it, because that's what God gave it to you for.' I guess that's a value I got from my granddaddy. Wanna hear one of my poems?"

I was stunned by this time—stunned that he was sharing this story, stunned that he wrote poems and wanted to recite one to me, stunned that this interview thing seemed to be working. He went on to recite his latest and a few others.

Then we went on to tell the stories of our childhood, our favorite memories, things people had told us to keep us in our place, ways we'd come into our own knowing and what we were doing with what we knew. Two hours passed and we were still there, drinking coffee, losing and finding ourselves in each others' stories.

What I learned that day about going first has changed everything. Now I know that the kind of conversations I crave don't happen by default. They happen when I take a risk and go first. Many of us hunger for a conversation that matters, but we wait for someone else to start it. It's scary to take that risk, so we pretend that communion doesn't matter, that we aren't interested in another's experience.

If that's the case, why do we enjoy overhearing conversations? Why are millions of viewers hooked on reality TV? How have some soap operas stayed on the air for fifty years? We love watching the human drama unfold. We're looking for reminders of what we once knew. Like sea turtles returning to the place of their birth, or penguins listening for the call of their mate. We're longing for connection, a sign that we matter, a story that reminds us it's the same way there.

Song: The Conversation (this is a conversation between my Muse and me)

You are my spirit and I call on you
to help me remember what I know
you are the flame that lights the path I walk
when my memory of our oneness starts to go
you are the force that keeps me moving on,
the guide whose hand I need to lead me home
take me in your arms and lead me through the dark
to the spring from which all healing waters flow

I am the one whose hand is in your hand
I will lead you down whatever path you choose
I am your guardian, I'm your dearest friend
I'm your deepest intuition, I'm your Muse
I am the voice that calls you to the Light,
the truest of the voices that you hear
and every time you call on me I'm there for you
I'm always at your side, I'm always near.

Then do you have the answers I am looking for?
All the answers that you seek, you have inside

How am I to know if what I choose is right?
If you've chosen out of love, love will abide
and when I feel the darkness of the world in me,
what am I to do with all my grief?
My child, your world is only what you say it is
If you call it dark then dark is what will be

How am I to know what I am here to do?
Just be who you are, the doing will get done
How can I get past the fear of what's to come?
All that fear will disappear once you've begun
How can I remember I am of the light
when there's hunger and hardship all around?
Take the hand of everyone you're walking with
and the love you feel will spread that light around.

Intimate conversations are masterful collaborations of two creators, each aware that giving is receiving and listening is an active verb. They can happen in a corporate cafeteria, on a train, in a living room, board room, or rest room. The Essene Gospel of Peace reminds us that "Only through the communions... will we learn to see the unseen, to hear that which can't be heard, and to speak the unspoken word." Our communions are the bridge from soul to soul, heaven to earth, dark to light. They are the way in and the way through, and all we need to do is go first.

NONE (3:00 PM)

Wake me from my sleep and rouse me
break through my dreams like a bird
Be the voice that guides me
Let your kindness flow through me day and night.

To become our own spiritual authority, we have to move and think and speak from our own personal knowing. Our power comes from our ability to transform what we have experienced into what we know. It's an alchemy of sorts, where we transmute the lead of our experience into the gold of our wisdom. Making a life is the process of converting our wisdom into action. Each of us knows what no one else knows because no one else has lived our lives, seen what we've seen, felt what we've felt. The great Persian poet Rumi writes, "The throbbing vein will take you further than any thinking." This is a great clue.

When you think of the people who have inspired you, changed your thinking, altered the course of your life, are they not the ones who spoke and lived from the heart? Are they not the ones who stand before you with the courage to be simply who they are, to share their visions, their struggles, their fears? This is the stuff of spiritual authority—this transparency, this risking, this willingness to say "It's a new frontier here, and not one of us has a map, but with what we know together, we can surely make it."

As we proceed along the path of inner self-management, structural changes occur within us that allow a significant increase in the level of indwelling spirit and this, in turn, appears as a significant increase in one's level of consciousness. William Tiller, physicist

VESPERS (SUNSET)

With tears in my eyes I behold you
Every place that I turn, you are there
In the wars, in the floods, in the earthquakes
Through our hands do we bring you to life.

Theism is the belief that one God, personal and omnipotent, created and rules the world and humans. The term derives from the Greek *theos* meaning God. It was first used by Ralph Cudworth in the 1600s. It is conjectured that theism emerged to help our ancestors survive the trauma of self-consciousness and the shock of non-being. They came up with the concept of God to help them deal with their awe, their powerlessness over death, their wonder at the beauty and vastness of the universe. All that they could not perceive as belonging to themselves they projected outward onto the Supreme Being they called God. God was the Creator of all things, the controller of all things, the force behind all great powers. God, understood theistically, is a human construct.

> *The courage to take meaninglessness into itself presupposes a relation to the ground of being which we have called "absolute faith." It is without a special content, yet it is not without content. The content of absolute faith is the "god above God." Absolute faith and its consequence, the courage that takes the radical doubt, the doubt about God, into itself, transcends the theistic idea of God.* Paul Tillich, theologian

Waking up is a process of finding ourselves, listening to ourselves, our thoughts, our bodies. This the work of the soul—to discover what is true and align ourselves with that. To experience every tragic and terrible thing knowing that it holds a lesson for us. To know that what we think has an effect on how we feel, that what we feel has an effect on what is, that our thoughts and words are the tools with which we forge our lives.

Many of us don't even know how we feel about something until long after it has happened. We've been so conditioned to how we "should" feel and act, that it's hard to separate what we "should" be feeling from what we actually *do* feel. Waking up is the first step in turning that around. It's taking time to breathe before we speak. It's sitting down every once in a while and locating our feelings, noticing which way they're pulling us, giving them our love and attention.

Waking up is also knowing we are *not* our feelings. We are the one observing them, tending to them, finding ways to release them and keep our energy flowing. They are not us. They are transient, passing through. We don't become them any more than the mirror becomes what it reflects. We can throw black paint at the sky all we want, but the sky will not change colors. To be awake is to have a mind like sky, untainted by the particularities of any event.

William James wrote that "the greatest revolution in our generation is that human beings, by changing the inner attitudes of their minds, can change the outer aspects of their lives." If we feel like we're in the middle of a nightmare, we don't have to stay there. We can wake ourselves up, get to the bottom of what's scaring us, see what illusion or expectation we've brought to the table. We can check to see if we ventured off into the past or the future, then get back to being in the present moment.

To be awake is to be constantly rearranging our inner attitudes, shape-shifting our thoughts as we become mindful of their power. The contours of our lives are shaped by our thoughts, molded by our speaking. We are the inventors of our own reality, and every relationship, every meeting, encounter, email and text message is a canvas, a stage upon which we create and express ourselves.

How many of us experience work as something we have to do in order to buy ourselves time on the weekends for our real lives? How many of us put in our time, but hold ourselves back, as if to be fully alive, fully joyful and intimate and creative in the workplace would diminish our supply for later? The other day, a woman in the armed services was interviewed on National Public Radio about preparing for war with her fellow soldiers, "Finally our lives have meaning now—they don't just revolve around what we do all day." If it takes a national disaster or a war for us to feel that our lives are meaningful, something is terribly wrong.

Disaster originally meant *out of touch with the stars*—but look at us now. We are out of touch with ourselves, out of touch with our neighbors, out of touch with the meaning of our connection to others around the globe. Out of touch with the potential we have to be inspired artists creating from our own personal and deep wisdom. Studies reveal that most peoples' worst dread is the thought of having lived a meaningless life, but what is it that gives our life meaning? It's connection, community, a sense that the part we play matters to the whole.

In the course of a day, there are many opportunities to feel powerless, many occasions in which we feel less the actor and more the acted upon. In the workaday world, there is often pressure to produce, a false sense of urgency, a mentality of scarcity, a tendency to overcomplicate things and make unreasonable demands on people. It is our job to stay balanced in the face of this.

COMPLINE (9:00 P.M.)

Into your arms I commend my spirit
though I sleep you continue to breathe
I give thanks for this day and this lifetime
I give thanks that you hold me this night.

Recognize what is before your eyes and the mysteries will be revealed to you. For there is nothing hidden that will not be revealed. Gospel of Thomas

I gave a talk at a hospital the other night, introducing an exhibition of photographs done by a group of doctors. A couple of them were in a snit, wondering why I'd been invited as the speaker. For some reason, they were uneasy with the fact that I'd written a book called *God Is at Eye Level—Photography as a Healing Art*. They grumbled about this to the woman who invited me to talk, and she called me saying, "You might want to soft-pedal the God part and the healing part. These guys are just hobbyists. They say their photographs don't have anything to do with healing."

I arrived early enough to view all their photographs and was deeply moved by their images of the Himalayas, Canyon de Chelly, a barrio in San Diego, close-ups of flowers and children and animals, black and white studies in shadow and depth. They were incredible images and had a powerful impact, especially since many brought back memories of some of my favorite places.

When I started my talk, I was careful to speak only for myself, sharing with the audience how photography is a healing experience for me, how it calms my soul, keeps me in the present moment, gives me a sense of being one with the Divine. I speak freely about spiritual matters all the time, and never edit my words or feelings about the sacredness of life. So when I commented on their images, referring to each doctor's work and how it specifically affected me, altered my awareness, conjured up memories and meaning, I wove in words like holy, healing, the Divine, oneness, commonness—and I saw some of those doctors move to the edge of their seats with tears in their eyes.

No one had ever spoken about their work before. No one ever said concretely, this is how it mattered to me, this is where it took me, this is how it made me feel and what it made me think of. This is why I think it's holy, healing work.

At the end of the talk, every one of those doctors came up to me privately and acknowledged how proud they felt to have their work referred to as spiritual. One after the other, they said things like, "You know, you can't use the G word in the office, but I think you're absolutely right...I'm glad you said that. I believe it, but you can't let people know that...Thanks for talking about my work like you did. I could never say those things. You have to watch what you say, you know."

I felt a little sadness driving home. That men like that—educated, talented, in the helping professions, and several of them close to retirement—had caved in to the notion that it's not OK to reveal your inner self. Not one of them would dare to speak of the holy in the workplace, but they loved when someone else did. My going first, it opened up something for them. I'll never know what or how it matters, but I know it did some good that night.

The ultimate and highest leave-taking is leaving God for GOD, leaving your notion of God for an experience of that which transcends all notions.

Meister Eckhart

I don't need a personal God
to be grateful for my life
and all that's in it.

I don't need to feel that Some One
fashioned me with His Own Hands,
knows all the hairs on my head
jerks His knee in response to
my every prayer.

I don't need pearly gates,
fires of Hell, vestal virgins
to live right, to give this opportunity
of a *lifetime* my whole devotion.

I am not in training
for some other time
to satisfy some Other Being.
I am here to make lighter
the burdens of everyone
I stumble upon
and to those across the seas
to whom I'm connected
like hand to mouth.

Then why, I wonder,
do I call out so often,
O God this, O God that,
like God is on the other end of the line
waiting for me alone?

My brain and my heart
are two rivers
running their own course
on the way to the Sea of Everything.

One knows, one feels,
One is the elder, one the child.
It's only when they fuse
that the God of the Heavens
explodes into light and becomes my way.

After reading the first chapter of this book, my Mom asked, "Do you really think there's something to this evolutionary stuff?"

I said, "Mom, in 1976 when I came out to you, you told me never to tell Dad or I'd be responsible for him dying of a heart attack. Would you say that if I came out to you now?"

"No."

"And in 1980 when I was in my militant-angry feminist phase and stopped shaving my legs, you wrote me a letter saying how selfish I was. Didn't I know I was an embarrassment to my brother and sister when their friends saw my hairy legs? Would you say that to me now?"

"No, of course not."

"And in 1981, when Dad disowned me for living in the same house with a man, you went along with him and refused to let me come home. Would you do that now?"

"No, I'd stand up to him. He was wrong to do that."

"That's what I mean by evolutionary. You have advanced your consciousness over the years. You have grown yourself up spiritually. You've taken responsibility for your own thoughts and decisions. You're your own authority now."

"Oh, I get it," she says. "OK, hurry up and finish it. I can't wait to read the next chapter."

True spiritual practice springs from, not toward, enlightenment. Our practice does not lead to unity consciousness—it is unity consciousness.

Jiddu Krishnamurti (1895-1986)

DISCIPLINE

There are different ways of looking at the word "discipline." One brings to mind spankings, standing in the corner, boot camp. Another, more tender reading brings to mind the word "disciple," one who passes along spiritual wisdom. That is the one we are talking about here. We are training ourselves to be evolutionary, ecumenical carriers of wisdom. Training ourselves to BE the light we want to see in the world. And in order to turn on our light and shine, we have to know two things: where the switch is and how to increase the wattage. All that is part of our spiritual practice, which is the foundation for evolutionary creativity.

Our spiritual practice tones our mindfulness muscles, just as a physical discipline might tone your abs. The results of mindfulness are tranquility, compassion, spiritual and social awareness, balance, bliss. I could go on. All this is guaranteed, but there is a minimal requirement. Daily practice. Hence, the word discipline.

I don't know why human beings are reluctant to commit to this, especially when the rewards are so satisfying, but I do know we are. I myself reluctantly started a spiritual practice in 1990 when my good friend reminded me that unless I committed to that, things would never work out as I wanted them to.

I was in graduate school at Syracuse University, on the verge of quitting, when I called her for a consult. I told her how out of place I felt, how I was old enough to be everyone's mother, how the students cared more about spring breaks and Cancun than anything we were there to learn. I felt like an outcast.

She asked me three questions, and those three questions changed the course of my life. "Are you eating and drinking moderately?" No, I confessed, admitting to drinking lots of Chardonnay and having a stash of Almond Joy miniatures in all my pockets.

"What are you doing for your body—are you working out?"

"No. Nothing."

"What about a spiritual practice. Do you have a spiritual practice?"

"No."

"Jan, don't make any decisions about quitting school right now. Your life cannot work right if you don't have those three things taken care of. Take two weeks to get it together, then call me back."

I went out and bought a bicycle and started biking to school. I limited my wine to the weekends and threw out all my little Almond Joys. Then I thought about a spiritual practice. I wasn't going to do anything uncomfortable, I knew that. What I decided on was twenty minutes of silence before a lighted candle every morning. No phones, no magazines, no newspapers. Just the fire, me, and my cup of coffee.

I was a little edgy at the beginning, but settled into the practice within a few days. By week two, I extended the time to thirty minutes. I wasn't trying to control my thoughts or get from one place to another. I was simply opening my mind like a satellite dish to Intelligence–at-Large, and the signals came in loud and clear. If I got distracted, I simply focused on my breathing to get back on center and the whole process was quite exhilarating. I felt inspired, balanced, and more myself somehow.

When two weeks was up and I called Paula back, I was like a new person.

"Paula, you're not going to believe it, everyone on campus has changed dramatically!"

She laughed, knowing that no one had changed but me, and that change made all the difference. I stayed on to finish graduate school and have maintained my spiritual practice for 20 years, knowing it's what keeps me rooted and immune from stress. I have aged in the process like a fine wine, and now devote much more time to my practice of silence.

Research studies show that more of our brain lights up when we attach ourselves to the Infinite, so it's no surprise that a spiritual practice leads to higher levels of creativity, intuition and productivity. When we limit our reception of noisy information and open ourselves to the silence of Intelligence-at-Large, we stop feeling overwhelmed by petty facts and experience the birth of immense possibilities. Being connected with Supreme Intelligence means continuing renewal, constant upgrading of our creative consciousness.

We have disciplined ourselves to fasten our seatbelts, to put children in car carriers, to stop smoking, for the most part, and these external disciplines promote our well-being. This discipline of interior practice promotes the well-being of our spirit and bodymind. And since we are to love others as we love ourselves, this is one way of fully loving ourselves. Attaining permanent enlightenment is beyond our reach, but to practice and express our awakening—this is being a light in the world.

You are saturated with innate natural perfection. Buddha

MATINS (MIDNIGHT)

I awaken and light the candle
I ready myself for your love
Toward bliss do I move as you breathe me
Hymns of praise do I sing all day long.

Adoration is the essential preparation for right action. Evelyn Underhill

We heal ourselves in the state of mindfulness by being present to the moment at hand. When we stand in the midst of what is, we are released from the yoke of what has been, detached from the fear of what might be. There is only the moment, our awareness, the Light of Life flowing through us as we breathe. All is peace in the eternal Now.

We are vulnerable to fear only when we leave the present. If I drift into the past, my regrets surge up, my memories of failing and forsaking. If I shift into the future, I meet with doubt and discouragement, anxiety about what's to come, what I'm not capable of controlling. It's in the present moment that I belong. Only there do I feel my balance.

We are yanked backward and forward by our earthly concerns, torn away from our center, from the calm of the moment. Whether dwelling on old pain, or fearing the unknown, we detach from our power source and lose our steam. Only through awareness do we can escape this vortex; only through vigilance do we keep ourselves present and resist the seduction of past and future.

People who learn to control their inner experience will be able to determine the quality of their lives, which is as close as any of us come to being happy.
                                                     Mihaly Csikszentmihalyi

There never was a more holy age than ours, and never a less...there is no less holiness at this time than there was the day the Red Sea parted. Annie Dillard

Dear Maker of Light,
Thank you for your presence in my life.
You are the constant
the one great mystery
the One to whom I could be no nearer.

What I breathe, that is you
What I hope for, that is you
What I create and call forth and celebrate,
you, you, you.
In that space between my candle and me,
fully invisible
there you are.

In the breeze that rattles my bedroom blinds,
in the sparrow's song,
the red of the rose, the blue of my eye
there you are, again and again.

How does it happen people think you are distant?

In the marrow of my bones,
in the throb of my heart,
the wet of my tear, the burst of my laughter,
Only you. Only you.
Only you.

An older monk tells a younger one: "I have finally learned to accept people as they are. Whatever they are in the world, a prostitute, a prime minister, it is all the same to me. But sometimes I see a stranger coming up the road and I say, 'Oh, Jesus Christ, is it you again?'"

We attract experiences supporting our deepest beliefs. What are yours? What beliefs are you ready to discard? Think of a recent event and see if you can connect it to a belief that you hold.

God is the Universe
and is ever expanding
soon, scientists of the future
will not be able to detect the start of it all—
the Big Bang—
because we will have expanded too far ahead
to track back to the beginning.

The explosion of intelligence in the cosmos—
that happening we call God—
is happening day and night,
moment by moment,
as stardust forms itself into planets,
stars burst into supernovas,
galaxies self-organize
and humans create the story of
what in the world is going on.

Intelligence—God's DNA—filters down
from its original light
and is transformed into food
for all plants and animals.
We eat God at every meal.
We metabolize God
in the living of our lives-
our choices, our risks, our sufferings-
all part of the universe
expanding through us.

Are you embarrassed
by the pettiness of your concerns yet?

Each of us is contributing daily to the creation of our common future, for better or worse, through our images, words, actions, and works. The more awareness we bring to the task, the more useful, the more compelling are our creations. The capacity to reach the highest states of awareness through contemplation, compassion, and grace is not limited to clerics, sages, saints. Any one of us can embark on that journey, find divinity in every detail, commit to dissolving dualities and experiencing oneness in our own minds and lives.

If we want to live in beauty, we must drop what is not beautiful from our minds. When you close your eyes to focus on something beautiful, where do you go? What image do you see? What is it about that place that brings you joy?

How do we open ourselves to insight into the deepest levels of reality? By dropping the limitations of ordinary thinking and feeling in our bodies our connectedness to all life. If we want to live in truth, we must question every belief we cling to and let go of whatever insults our souls. If we want to know and experience oneness with the Divine, with others, in ourselves, we must give up our dualities, our fragmented thinking and dare to endanger our prior assumptions. There is *not* the sacred and the profane, the earthly and the heavenly, the sinners and the saved. There is only The One Thing, infusing and infused into everything. The mystics in every tradition have been guiding us toward this awareness for centuries.

My eyes are the eyes through which God sees. They are the eyes through which God sees his own body. Vilyat Inayat Khan.

What we are looking for is Who is looking. St. Francis of Assisi

He is at the same time the One who reveals Himself and that through which He manifests himself. Sufi master Ibn al Arabi

As we go about creating our lives, our words and actions transform into the world we belong to, the world we are shaping. As the food we eat becomes our bodies, so do our expressions become the world. We are living in a country that was once just a thought in the imaginations of a few men. We go to work in buildings that were conceived in thought; we listen to music, watch movies, read books that are concrete manifestations of someone's feelings and passions. And these creations touch our hearts, change our minds, move us to action. Energy becomes matter, matter becomes energy, and our hearts are the crucible where the transformation occurs. It is where the creator and created give rise to each other.

Prayer is not a stratagem for occasional use, a refuge to resort to now and then. It is rather like an established residence for the innermost self. All things have a home: the bird has a nest, the fox has a hole, the bee has a hive. A soul without prayer is a soul without a home. Abraham Joshua Heschel

LAUDS (SUNRISE)

They claim that you live in the heavens
though I feel you inside like a sun
burning away my falsehoods
till all that I am is your truth.

Two children found a bag containing twelve marbles. They argued over how to divide the toys and finally went to see the Mulla. When asked to settle their disagreement, the Mulla asked whether the children wanted him to divide the marbles as a human would or as Allah would.

The children replied, "We want it to be fair. Divide the marbles as Allah would."

So, the Mulla counted out the marbles and gave three to one child and nine to the other.

Meditation:
This can be practiced in just a few minutes, so try to incorporate it as a part of your daily life. Come into a comfortable seated position on the floor or in a chair. Sit with the back flat, crown of the head lifted, shoulders relaxed, and chest open. Rest your hands in the lap or on the knees. Close your eyes, deepen the breath and release any thoughts from the mind. Gently repeat the following softly out loud or in your mind:

May I be safe from all danger
May I be held in the arms of God
May I be strong in spirit and body
May I be true to my heart and soul.

Repeat the phrases again, changing "May I" to "May you" while you think of a specific person, or of a group of people, or of the whole planet.

Finish with a few slow, deep breaths, feeling compassion, love, and kindness flowing through your body. Take a moment or two before moving on with the rest of your day.

Until one is committed, there is hesitancy, the chance to draw back, always ineffectiveness. Concerning all acts of initiative (and creation) there is one elementary truth, the ignorance of which kills countless ideas and splendid plans: that the moment one definitely commits oneself, then Providence moves too. All sorts of things occur to help one that would never otherwise have occurred. A whole stream of events issues from the decision, raising in one's favor all manner of unforeseen incidents and meetings and material assistance, which no one could have dreamed would have come their way.

I have learned a deep respect for Goethe's couplets:

"Whatever you can do or dream you can, begin it.
Boldness has genius, power, and magic in it."

W. H. Murray, *The Scottish Himalayan Expedition*

PRIME (6:00 A.M.)

I call out your name night and day
like a young bride I stand at the gate
in the garden your scent surrounds me
at the well do I draw you up.

Child psychologist Chilton Pearce says that our feelings of limitation are shaped by the trinity of culture, myth, and religion. He writes: "We actually contain a built-in ability to rise above restriction, incapacity, or limitation, and as a result of this ability, possess a vital adaptive spirit that we have not yet fully accessed. While this ability can lead us to transcendence, paradoxically it can lead also to violence; our longing for transcendence arises from our intuitive sensing of this adaptive potential and our violence arises from our failure to develop it." This thought is consistent with the words of Jesus spoken in the Gospel of Thomas, "If you bring forth what is within you, what you bring forth will save you. If you do not bring forth what is within you, what you do not bring forth will destroy you." Our religions and culture have conditioned us toward a deadly passivity that has kept us from bringing forth what is within us, from accessing and expressing that vital spirit within. We have created a life system that has not only outgrown its usefulness, but is actually keeping us from evolving into our next phase of consciousness—the recognition of our own divinity. The violence that is erupting all over this planet is arising out of our failure to create, to shape our lives and our culture with the tools of illumined imagination.

In the Islamic tradition, people are encouraged to let their words pass through "the three gates" before speaking. *Is it true? Is it kind? Is it necessary?* If it doesn't pass this test, it ought not be spoken.

Spend a day paying close attention to everything that comes out of your mouth. Listen carefully to your words and notice if you are saying things you would not want to come true. Practice speaking as if your life was a materialization of your words. Do this until you become aware of every word that you speak.

Morning Psalm 101

Yea, though I look out at cedars and oak
see your face in their branches and leaves
though I walk by day through forests of spruce
by night do I long for the touch of your hand.

I run to the water through mists of dawn
howling like a wolf as she calls her mate
leaping like a fawn on wobbly legs
in the woods of my heart do I seek you.

What is this game I play all day?
This hide and seek from dawn till dusk?
I see your breath in the winter air,
hear your voice in the running stream
I am not looking for what is not there
I am in union with that which I seek.

I walked into the classroom to facilitate the first session of a six-week series
on Evolutionary Creativity. Instead of giving them my definition of the concept,
I had them split into four groups and each come up with their own definition of
what would define evolutionary creativity.

After fifteen minutes of sharing, we surfaced their ideas. The first group said
that a defining characteristic of evolutionary creativity would be that it was
connected to the Infinite, rooted in the sacred, or in harmony with the person's
deepest commitments.

The second group said it was a creative energy that could dance with chaos,
tangle with turbulence. That to be evolutionary, we must be able to deal with
the troublesome aspects of being pushed to our edges and nudged toward the
new.

The third group said to be evolutionary, a creative work must take the whole
into account, be a force for good, a gift and a contribution to humanity itself.

And the last group said it would inspire action. The creation itself would be
an energizing force that would cause the beholder to act in response.

As we discussed the idea further, we realized that it is hard to define it, but you'd know it when you saw it because you'd feel it deep inside you and you'd never be the same. The question came up whether Georgia O'Keefe was an evolutionary creator. Some thought yes. Some thought no. And the upshot was that we can never know the impact of someone's creative work as each of us responds uniquely to the creations of others.

We can say of ourselves we are evolutionary creators if our creations meet the requirements of the time: to be steeped in commitment to a greater good and to inspire others to find their voice and release their power.

All parts seek the whole
And I am no different
You O Source and Morning Light
You O Thundering Rainmaker
You O Invisible Plenitude
My thoughts are the sign of you,
even as they doubt
or occasionally deny you.

O Great Mystery, Vast Wonder
It is you in me that renders
this freedom to think beyond you

Thank you for the chance
to give life a whirl, knowing
when it's over I'll fold back in
to Thought itself
drift back home to Mind-at-Large.

TERCE (9:00 A.M.)

My head is bowed in reverence
My knees are bent in prayer
everywhere, every minute I feel you
there is nowhere that you are not.

Just as in earthly life lovers long for the moment when they are able to
breathe forth their love for each other, to let their souls blend in a soft whisper,
so the mystic longs for the moment when in prayer he can, as it were, creep
into God. Søren Kierkegaard

The other day, I was photographing tide pools at the ocean's edge. The waves crashed onto the shore, ruffled their way across the rocks, and swirled and bubbled into the shallow, sandstone pools beneath my feet. I hovered over a patch of moss-covered rock and photographed a piece of the action. When the photos were developed, I could hardly believe my eyes. Every single tiny bubble I caught in my lens reflected back an image of myself. Everything I looked at looked back at me and contained me.

All life is a mirror to us, reflecting who we are back to ourselves. If we look deeply enough into a redwood or mountain stream, into a person's face, the petal of an iris, the eyes of a kitten, we will find ourselves there. We will recognize our oneness, our common ground—the life force that holds us all together on this plane. And it is the *seeing* that is Divine—the looking, the recognizing, the awareness of oneness that *is* the One.

Stop what you're doing and take ten deep breaths. Breathe deeply enough so you feel your stomach inflating like a balloon on the in breath. Breathe in through your nose and out through your mouth, letting your breath be the singular thing you focus on.

Try breathing in to a count of four, holding your breath to a count of two, and exhaling slowly to a count of six. Do this during the day if you feel stressed.

When you pray, go into your room and shut the door. Matthew 6:6

Prayer is the contemplation of the facts of life from the highest point of view.
Ralph Waldo Emerson

We are intricately entwined with the Divine in ways that cannot be spoken of, but the reality is not to be denied. We do not have to seek after God. There is no journey to take, no texts to pore over, nothing to learn in the matter. As the Lankavatara Sutra reminds us, "These teachings are only a finger pointing to the Noble wisdom ... they are intended for the consideration and guidance of the discriminating minds of all people, but they are not Truth itself, which can only be self-realized within one's own deepest consciousness."

It is through us, through our consciousness, that the divinization of humanity and all the earth is occurring. By learning to see, by becoming alert and awake, we feel the call and presence of the Unmanifest guiding us into the creative action that gives birth to this process. Everything takes form according to the consciousness that shapes it. Since we create in our own image, in order for our creations to be light-filled and inspired, so must our self-image be. What comes out of us is only as brilliant, as loving as our images of ourselves. To give gold, we must mine the gold within.

The treasure is in us, of us. And if we think not, then our thoughts deceive us. It is like trying to solve a problem with a mindset that is the problem. We cannot be healed until we accept that we are healed. We cannot sense the Divine until we feel its presence in our own cells and devote our deepest love to the Life Within.

How we see ourselves has everything to do with how we see others and how we see God. As Anthony de Mello said, "If you have to have an image of God, make sure it's an image of the kindest, most loving person you know, because you are going to become your image of God."

SEXT (NOON)

I am a turbine to your wildness
stepping down the roar of you
that you might be experienced
as a breeze of relief
a glass of comfort on a hot summer day.

A friend of mine, Beth, filled her jeep with rocks from Home Depot in preparation for her weekend task of constructing a stone wall. Late that night, she remembered she was supposed to pick up two people from the airport early the next morning. She panicked at first, realizing there was no room for them or their luggage. Then the anxiety subsided, and a calm resolve took its place. She would get dressed, put on her work gloves, and unload those rocks one by one.

It was dark outside and there was no light to see by, so she just carried the rocks to the place she planned to build the wall. One on top of another, in the pitch black of night, she laid them down as orderly as she could. "It was as if time had stopped," she said. "Hours passed, but I had no sense of it. And though the rocks were big, they never felt heavy." After, when Beth emptied her Jeep, she went inside and went to bed, knowing it would soon be time to go to the airport.

That morning when she went outside to get in her car, she was stunned at what she saw. Her stone wall glistened in the early morning light, beautifully shaped and brilliantly designed, as if it had been put together by a master of the trade.

Spirit flows through our hands like a current through a stream. It is life-giving, light-filled power that pours out of us in our purest moments of love and compassion. And yet we hold back. We hold back tenderness, we hold back our power, we doubt our own ability to work miracles though Jesus himself said, "Any of the works I have done, you can do and more." It is our history that is holding us back—old voices, old ways—while today, this hour, this moment calls to us, "Wake up now! Everything, *everything* is in your hands."

If you are going to be my teacher
hone your memory like a razor
so your forgetting is rare
and doesn't overlap with mine.

If you are going to be my teacher
wake up polishing the mirror of your self
so when I sit at your feet, looking up
it is myself I see
my own torch burning and lighting the way.

If you are going to be my teacher
start practicing surgery so you can remove
my cancerous judgments
my deteriorating opinions
my tumors of cynicism and jealousy.

If you are going to be my teacher
take multiple vitamins
for your own intelligence
so you never forget
I am you too.

If you are going to be my teacher
get out your church key and open the can of me
then stand back and make room
for the shower of stars
that will fall your way
each one a question
and you its mark.

You start each day with a list of things to do. What if you made a list of Things Not to Do in order to get your other things done? What would go on that list?

When our souls materialize a body in order to do their work in this world, from the very beginning we are led to believe that we are our bodies. But we are *not* our bodies. We are their observers, their caretakers. We are the Mind behind their movements, the Eye behind their seeing. The cells in our bodies completely replace themselves every seven years, but our consciousness, connected to the Source, maintains its perfect wholeness throughout eternity. Our cells come and go, but our memory of the ocean stays the same.

Living creatively means diving into this fountainhead, this overflowing spring, and letting its freshness source and sustain us. Our souls have conjured these bodies to do their work in the world, and just as a pitcher of water floats in the river—water within, and water without—so do we hold within the very Divine to whom we belong. Ours is a holographic universe and in every part, the Whole is contained. The answers to our questions are in every cell, waiting to be expressed in the flow of our feelings. It is not intellect we need to fix our lives, our relationships, our broken world—it is insight, inner sight.

The universe is bound together in communion, each thing with all the rest. The gravitational bond unites all the galaxies, the electromagnetic interaction bonds all the molecules; the genetic information connects all the generations of the ancestral tree of life. We live in interwoven layers of bondedness.

Brian Swimme

NONE (3:00 PM)

I will leave the chaos behind me
to sit in your lap of love
to merge with you is my passion
to be one is all that I seek.

Dear Light of Day and Dark of Night,

Thank you for being me,
Powering me, guiding me
I am your hands and feet,
Your voice and ears,
I am a force of substance
a revealer, a transformer,
a healer and midwife.
I am your consort in creation
ground to your seed.
I am the matter
that you energize
I am water to your air
tangible and ever returning in every form.
Press outward and extend yourself
Seep out through my pores.
Be me and more
so your light shines through this darkness.

I worked once in a mall that sponsored a huge antique show. When I walked around to see what they had, my eyes landed on a pair of tiny black patent leather shoes lined with a stunning pink silk. They were just like *my* shoes, the ones I wore for Easter and dress-up occasions when I was three. My heart jumped when I saw them. Deep feelings stirred when I picked them up—not specific memories, but *feelings* from that time in my life. Cavernous feelings of wonder and curiosity about the world opening up in front of my eyes, ahead of me. Feelings of innocence, fearlessness, trust.

I bought those little shoes for the feelings they caused, the joy that welled up when I imagined myself in the shoes of a child again. One day I took those shoes and my camera to the playground, to the lake, to the church steps—and I photographed them in every environment. I placed the shoes in front of the bottom step to the big slide, at the water's edge, approaching the huge golden doors to the cathedral. Each time I did this, new feelings would rise up and I could access something old and true about myself, something untainted, un-touched by anything outside me. I felt my body like I felt it as a three year old. I was fully present, completely embodied. Feelings from forty years earlier came to life like a waking dragon coming out of a long slumber. I felt fearless again, in awe again.

When I packed my backpack for a trip around the world, I slipped those shoes in at the last moment. It seemed like a ridiculous thing to do, but in some way, they felt like my vehicle to wholeness, what some might call a transitional object that kept me in touch with a part of me I didn't want to lose. It wasn't that I was afraid to go without them—it was that there were places I wanted to go *with* them, in order to feel the fullness I sensed with them.

When I reached the base camp to the Himalayan Annapurna Sanctuary, I rose at dawn and placed the shoes on the ground before some of the world's most magnificent peaks. As the mauve tones of daylight crept over the horizon, a wild joy surfaced as I photographed those little shoes. I remembered myself. I was the little girl who had climbed the mountain. I was the one who had no fear, who was in the moment, who felt the breath of God in the blowing wind. I was safe, in the arms of the Mother, always cared for, never alone.

In some strange way, those shoes helped me. They transported me to my deepest desires, my earliest knowing. They revived feelings I had learned to suppress, and once I learned the secret of finding my feelings, I was free to let go of the patent leather shoes.

Trekking down the mountain, I came upon a mother bathing her young daughter at the village pump. The girl looked small enough, I thought, for the shoes to fit her. I reached into my pack and pulled them out, offering them to the mother when the bath was complete. With smiles and sign language, I did my best to say: "Have her try them on. If they fit, she can have them."

The girl's face lit up like the morning sun. She put one on and it fit her per-fectly. Then she climbed into the other one, strapped up the shiny straps and

danced with delight. The mother bowed over and over with gestures of gratitude, and I bowed back, over and over, thanking *her* for the chance to be of
use.

Every time I think of those shoes, it all comes back, and mostly what I cherish is knowing that I *can* reclaim my body. I *can* have those original feelings. I
just need to remember what it feels like to be three, to be walking again for the
first time. And to be conscious that the direction I move in is toward joy, toward
nature, toward that desire throbbing in the middle of my heart.

*Do not accept what you hear by report, do not accept tradition, do not ac-
cept a statement because it is found in your books, nor because it is in accord
with your belief, nor because it is the saying of your teacher. Be lamps unto
yourselves.* Buddha on his deathbed

Joshu asked Nansen: "What is the path?"
Nansen said: "Everyday life is the path."
Joshu asked: "Can it be studied?"
Nansen said: "If you try to study, you will be far away from it.'"
Joshu asked: "If I do not study, how can I know it is the path?'"
Nansen said: "The path does not belong to the perception world, neither
does it belong to the nonperception world. Cognition is a delusion and
noncognition is senseless. If you want to reach the true path beyond doubt,
place yourself in the same freedom as sky. You name it neither good nor not-
good."
At these words Joshu was enlightened.

*We cannot know God until we know our own soul, and the soul is both sub-
stance and sensuality. Sensuality is the miracle of the incarnation through which
we are oned to the Trinity.* Julian of Norwich

VESPERS (SUNSET)

Wherever I am, you are there
yours is the breath in my lungs
Blow through me like a reed flute
To the world I will play your song.

We are not here to transcend life, but to be fully immersed in it. Our bodies are not something we must triumph over. They are the medium of our transformation, the cauldron in which the elements of heaven and earth are steeped until they transmute one day into the Being of which we are now the embryo. The journey we are on is a journey to fulfill this destiny, and we accomplish it through remembering our true nature, not through learning. We accomplish it by being true to our instincts, by listening to the wisdom of our bodies, and by abandoning all notions of separateness and other.

This is the great challenge upon us, and it is revolutionary work. It calls for extraordinary heroism in the realm of the everyday. It calls for us to take a stand. To stop colluding in the darkness of duality, to stop trafficking in negativity, and to let out, once and for all, over and over, the light within. To separate ourselves from multiplicity, to reveal the good news of the kingdom all around us, we must act on the basis of what we feel and know from our own experience.

A Zen student goes to the temple to become enlightened.
"I want to join the community and attain enlightenment. How long will it take
me?" he asks.
"Ten years," says the Master.
"How about if I work very hard and double my efforts?"
"Twenty years."

Double Entry Accounting

Yours, the heavens, the mysteries, the seeds
Mine, the earth, the awe, the sowing

Yours, the soul, the living, the dying.
Mine, the body, the meaning, the mourning

Yours, the day, the birdsong, the rainstorm
Mine, the gratitude, the laughter, the harvest

Yours, the Mind, the sea, the cosmos,
Mine, the thoughts, the sailing, the conscience

Yours, the hunger, the war, the earthquake
Mine, the feeding, the armistice, the rescuing

Yours, the breath, the eagle, the mountain
Mine, the words, the freedom, the climb

Yours, the sunset, the moon, the tide
Mine, the photograph, the song, the pearl

Yours, the forest, the seasons, the sky
Mine, the sap, the changing, the dew

Yours, me
Mine, You
Ours: the One, the Whole,
the All.

Song: Alphabet Mantra

Like the all in the oneness,
Like the branch and the vine
Like the call and the answer
Like the drink and the wine

Like the earth and the heavens
Like the forest and trees
Like the gate and the pathway
Like the hawk and the breeze

Like the iris and petals
Like the jewel and the mine
Like the known and the knowing
Like the laugh and the line

Like moonlight and darkness
Like nowhere and near
Like the oak and the acorn
Like pain and the tear

Like the quest and the seeker
Like rain and the flower
Like the sea and the islands
Like time and the hour

Like union and yearning
Like the vision and view
Like waves and the water
So I am to you.

So I am to you, Love, and you are to me
We dwell in each other, like salt and the sea.

COMPLINE (9:00 P.M.)

I am a ray of your golden sunshine
I am a spark from your endless fire
I am your Energy slowed down to matter
I am the particle born of your Wave.

Word spread across the countryside about the wise Holy Man who lived in a small house atop the mountain. A man from the village decided to make the long and difficult journey to visit him. When he arrived at the house, he saw an old servant inside who greeted him at the door. "I would like to see the wise Holy Man," he said to the servant. The servant smiled and led him inside. As they walked through the house, the man from the village looked eagerly around the house, anticipating his encounter with the Holy Man. Before he knew it, he had been led to the back door and escorted outside. He stopped and turned to the servant, "But I want to see the Holy Man!"

"You already have," said the old man. "Everyone you may meet in life, even if they appear plain and insignificant... see each of them as a wise Holy Man. If you do this, then whatever problem you brought here today will be solved."

Think about it: How is it we worship in the wrong direction looking upward instead of around to see who needs us?

Unless you start hearing your own voice no one can help you. Boddhidharma

A Zen master was asked what happens when we die.
"I don't know," he says.
"Aren't you a Zen master?"
"Yes, but not a dead one."

God, when he has just decided to launch upon his work of creation is called He. God in the complete unfolding Being, Bliss and Love, in which he becomes capable of being perceived by the reasons of the heart...is called You. But God, in his supreme manifestation, where the fullness of His Being finds its final expression in the last and all-embracing of his attributes, is called I.

14th century Cabbalist Moses de Leon

This is the kind of statement that can be known by the heart more easily than understood by the brain. It is ineffable, a deep mystery. Sit with it for awhile and see if you can feel it nestling into your heart. What is it trying to communicate to you?

Examination of Consciousness

Did you say only kind words today?
Did you remember your thoughts become your life?
Were you aware of your thoughts?
What was your first thought?
Did you have a prevailing emotion throughout the day?
What and why?
Did you remember that bliss is your natural state?
Did you feel it?
Did you say thank you as often as you were grateful?
Did you reveal your light?
Did you notice others' light?
Did you laugh out loud?
Did you sing?
Did you hug anyone?
Did you love your body?
Did you see yourself reflected in anyone?
Did you see God?
Are you thankful?
Did you say it?

At our last Evolutionary Creativity session, we went around the room to hear people's comments about what had changed for them over the six weeks. One woman said that she had always been kind of self-centered and had to constantly remind herself to ask about the well-being of others in her relationships.

"It just never occurred to me to ask about how other people were doing. I was so caught up in my own ideas. I had to write myself notes reminding me to talk less about myself and ask more open-ended questions," she said. "But since this class, I find that I'm doing it more naturally now. I'm aware of my actual oneness with others, so I don't have to work at it. Tuning into their issues is like tuning into my own now."

Another woman of German descent said she often felt a split down her middle. Half the time she was an assertive, direct person who spoke her mind easily, even to the point of intimidating others. She was an engineer by profession. The other half of the time she was an artistic jeweler who made beautiful art but was afraid of sharing it, feeling shy and hesitant to reveal this part of herself.

"After this class, I feel that the two parts of me have moved closer together," she said. "I don't feel so shy about my art anymore and it is easier for me to connect with others for more meaningful and casual conversations. I feel more whole, somehow."

In my opinion, this was the result of them having created new neural networks because of the discipline and consciousness they maintained throughout the six weeks. We all rewired our brains in some way, but for these two, it was actually apparent and able to be articulated.

This is how we evolve ourselves forward, how we upgrade our corrupt software — through dedication and commitment to higher levels of thinking and being. They are both free in ways they were not free before, and more conscious of the integration of heart and brain in their daily lives.

Whatever you do will be insignificant, but it is very important that you do it.

Mahatma Gandhi (1869-1948)

CREATIVITY
AND THE NEW COSMOLOGY

We're like caterpillars getting close to the Great Transformation. In preparation for its metamorphosis, the caterpillar eats 100 times its weight, falls asleep, and then forms a chrysalis. When the first imaginal cells of the butterfly begin to form themselves, the immune system of the caterpillar tries to fight them off. The immune system fails, and the caterpillar cells become the soup that nourishes the emerging butterfly.

We, as humans, are going through a similar process. We're in a massive consumption phase now, and many of us are asleep, napping in the chrysalis. Since we're all at different stages, some of us are feeling the invasion of "the new" and are resisting it with all our might. We don't want to give up what we know and have. Even though we're participating in a civilization that keeps millions of people starving while a small percentage own most of the wealth, we don't want the upset that fixing that might cost us. Even though most of our institutions are failing us, we don't have enough moral outrage to fuel a change in course. We've stuffed ourselves—those of us who can—and we're sleeping now. It's just too bad about the others.

In order to sustain this thinking, we have to tune out our emotions, because if we let ourselves *feel* our oneness with those people who have nothing because of this imbalance, then we'd have to *do* something. We'd have to bear the weight of our complicity. We'd have to feel the sorrow, and the hunger, and the angst, and the terror of the ones left behind. We'd have to cry, we'd have to forgive ourselves, and we'd have to act in different ways.

So instead we come up with all the rationalizations for not letting in the emotions. We live half-lives, buying more and more to make ourselves feel better, as if joy were something that comes from outside instead of bubbling up from within as a reward for being true. No, if we are to find real meaning, feel real joy, it will come on the wings of a fully engaged life, a life in the service of more than our self. It will come when we remember that giving is receiving, and the more we share ourselves, the more meaning and joy will come our way. Our spiritual traditions have tried to encourage this—"what you do for the least of these, you do unto me"—but we have failed to connect with the potency of the message.

We were born into the myth of one God in the heavens who created the universe in six days, rested on the seventh, and now spends all his time granting or turning down our prayers. We've seen the image of God and Adam on the Sistine Chapel ceiling and the masterpiece is branded onto our imagination. *The images on which we feed govern our lives,* according to mythopoetic author and Jungian analyst Marion Woodman, and the myth behind this image lies behind our worldview.

But this mythology no longer serves us and is giving way to a new revelation, a new cosmology that is relevant to these times and our evolved consciousness. It worked fine at the time Isaiah was a prophet, 700 years before the Common Era, when word had it God was punishing Israel for the nation's unfaithfulness. It worked as well for a medieval world that believed it would take 8000 years at 40 miles per day by mule to reach the sphere of the stars. It even held up in the 17th century when Bishop James Ussher, based on calculations from Genesis, announced that the creation of heaven and earth occurred on October 23, 4004 BCE.

But at a time when we can trace the lineage of the cosmos back 14 billion years, when we have sculptures from the period 200,000-500,000 BCE (the Berekhat Ram and the Venus of Tan Tan), when science informs us that 10% of our body weight consists of elementary hydrogen nuclei that came out of the Big Bang, and when more people are acquiring the ability to destroy the planet with nuclear weapons, we are seeing our relationship to the cosmos through a brand news lens. Now that humans have created the means to destroy the world, it is unconscionable to collude in a story that sees God as the creator of circumstances and humans as the victims, God as Geppetto and people as Pinnocchio.

The Sistine Chapel of the future might be a mirror, reflecting the part we each play in ongoing creation. Human beings, through the powers of our creative imaginations and unified consciousness, are re-pairing the opposites, transcending the dualities that have kept us separate from nature, from the Divine, and from each other. What is spiritual is the relationship between our cosmos and our mind.

We are coming to understand ourselves as expressions of the universe, activities of the cosmos. We are the universe reflecting back on itself, evolution pondering its next moves. We are the first ones—*homo sapiens*— to recognize the future is largely in our hands. It is happening *through* us, not *to* us. We are collaborating in the ever expanding cosmos by expressing creatively the ineffable mystery that surrounds us, sustains us, enlightens and sanctifies us. In the Huichol myth, Grandfather is Fire and Grandmother is Growth—an image quite different from the ones we've inherited.

It is blasphemous for any of us to say "I am not creative." All we *do* is create. We have desires and we create experiences from our desires. We have experiences and we create stories about those experiences. We hear the stories of others, and we are moved to tell our own, turn them into songs or poems or youtube movies. We wake up every day to an empty canvas of twenty-four hours and every night we go to bed having created our masterpiece for the day. We can do this consciously or unconsciously, but we all do it nevertheless. And the ones who are conscious of it are the ones most actively engaged in the work of evolution, of unification, of ongoing cosmic revelation.

Our culture is in deep trouble and everybody knows it. Every institution is in its death throes. Half the world's scientists are engaged in war research. Religions insist on separating humans from God and humans from their earthiness. Capitalism has begotten a greed that is growing like a malignant tumor as we globalize our pathologies. People are returning to fundamental beliefs so they won't have to sort through the complexities of social matters and form their own opinions. Churches are silencing the prophets and absolving the perpetrators of crimes against children.

A culture can't lift itself out of dark and destructive mindset, but creative acts and ideas from a few can ignite the moral imagination of the many. Look at Egypt. Our imaginations are the most potent engines of change in the universe. They are the receptors for Supreme Intelligence, incubators for evolutionary creativity. It is through the imagination that our thoughts become our lives, our lives become our stories, and our stories become bridges to higher consciousness and ultimate union.

The Bible's prophets were not intellectuals or theologians, they were story-tellers. They painted pictures for people, wove exotic tales for people, created metaphors that were consistent with the cosmology of the 3rd millennium before the Christian Era. They did a great job for their era, and now it's time for us to do our part in creating a spirituality that works with the 21st century cosmology. It's time to call God home, reconnect ourselves to the natural world, and proclaim the good news that as people on earth we share a single origin, a single community and a single destiny. The Creative Force is communicating its design to all people simultaneously, just as our DNA is communicating its genetic information to all our cells at every moment.

As photosynthesis came forth to enable the planet to evolve biologically, so too are we experiencing the emergence of a new phenomenon that is enabling the planet to evolve consciously. We ourselves are agents of a new transformation, engaged in a process of "infosynthesis" whereby we convert intelligence into inspiration through the creative power of our imagination. Through our spiritual practice (interior) and creative expression (exterior) we unite the opposites of spirit and matter which results in a combustion of original thinking and inspired action.

Every mystic and prophet alive today understands that their interests are not separate from anyone else's. Healing the wounds of the world is an act of self-interest. Mother Earth is healing herself through us. Every activity we engage in is both an activity of the universe and a human activity. The catastrophes of the times—the collapse of the economy, the failures of our institutions, the ineptness of war as a solution to any problem—all signs of a planetary mid-course correction. The earth as an organism will evolve, with or without us.

The universe itself is the primary revelation of the Divine and it is continuing to unfold through our thoughts, words, lives, and creations. The Divine speaks through Nature, Nature speaks through us, and the sacred is communicated through our rituals and relationships. Like the whole world in a grain of sand, revelation is enfolded and unfolding in all directions.

Our conversations are not *about* the Divine—our conversations *are* the Divine. We are awash in the Mystery, saturated in sacredness. This is the awareness that will bring us to our knees, stop us in our self-indulgent tracks and return us to our senses. This is the kind of spirituality that can *mean* something, lead to something that is poignant, personal, *passionate*. This is our chance to *BE* the ones we've been waiting for—to be prophetic, poetic mythmakers conspiring in the evolution of a conscious culture, a compassionate culture. As my mystic friend David says, "WE is just an acronym for Who Else?"

What does it matter
the myths of old
if they don't feed the soul
and fire us up
when we take them in?

What does it matter
if God exists or Jesus rose or
Eve ate an apple
if in our time we
allow hungry children,
human trafficking,
the shunning of gays
by the "people of God."

What do I care about church or religion
when they don't lead to justice
or mercy
or truth?

I am here to live out the meaning of God,
not to argue about what God means.

Don't make me laugh
with that pompous talk
about true religions.
Get up on your feet and *do* something.

Show me what it looks like to *be* a believer.

MATINS (MIDNIGHT)

Isaiah speaks: "The Lord GOD has given me a well-trained tongue,
that I might speak to the weary a word that will rouse them."
"You are gods," say the Psalms, "and all of you are children of the
most High." What more do we need to start creating,
to call forth words from the mouth of God?

Someone asked me what I thought was dying to be born. Homo sapiens, I said. Homo sapiens (Latin: *wise man* or *knowing man)* is dying to be born into the next iteration—the *homo sentiens,* perhaps. Homo sapiens *knows,* and homo sapiens sapiens even *knows that he knows,* but look where that's got us. Brains without a heart. *Homo sentiens* (Latin: *feeling human)* will bridge the brain-heart gap and compassion—*feeling with*— will be their modus operandi.

Homo sentiens will usher in cultures of kindness, economies of equity, politics of collaboration. They will rise up from the ashes of fallen institutions and imploded religions, bringing with them new myths and stories that heal and guide. They will honor creativity and see that every day is a canvas for every living being. They will be notorious for displays of adoration and awe, famous for crying at the drop of a hat—male and female both—and they will declare war obsolete once and for all.

Homo sentiens will revere the young and the aged. They will create communities where extraordinary education is common and ongoing, where people learn many languages, where food, health care and a decent home are available to everyone. They will have transcended religions and committed themselves to the common good with the greatest of faith. Children will be encouraged to make music, make art, and make culture. They will know their value from an early age as they will see this value reflected in every community's choices.

Homo sentiens will be aware of their oneness with the creation and the creatures and they will not distinguish between sacred and secular. All things will be holy in the eyes of these beings who are our descendants. Perhaps we will return one day in a *homo sentiens* body and will cry for joy. Alleluia! We see the light!

The American Astronomical Society informs us that the composition of the cosmos consists of 4% atoms and 96% dark matter or energy (which cannot be measured with current instruments.) Nothing outweighs everything by a huge margin. Physicist Michio Kaku explains the beginning of things: *Nothing became unstable and particles of Something began to form.*

Our Father, Holy Mother,
Creator of the Cosmos, Source of Life,
You are in my mind, in my garden,
in my cup of wine and loaf of bread.
Blessed be your names:
Mother, Allah, Goddess, Beloved, Father,
Radiant One, Yahweh, HaShem, Sophia
Your presence has come, your will is done
on earth as it is in the cosmos.

May we give each other strength, mercy,
tenderness, and joy
and forgive each other's failures,
silence, pettiness, and forgetfulness
as we ask to be forgiven
by those we've hurt.

Lead us home
to ourselves, to You,
to clarity, to oneness
and deliver us from the darkness
of our ignorance and fear.

So we pray and so we receive. Amen

In the region of nature, which is the region of diversity, we grow by acquisition; in the spiritual world, which is the region of unity, we grow by losing ourselves, by uniting. Rabindranath Tagore

Once, in India, I was on a train riding in a Ladies Compartment with three women and two children. We had plenty of extra room. When an elderly woman and her daughter appeared in the doorway, I motioned for them to come in. The other women in the compartment seemed perturbed, pursing their lips and shaking their heads with tight little movements. No one moved over to make room. Instead, they cast their eyes down and pretended not to notice the two women looking for seats.

Finally I stood up and took the older woman's hand, leading her to my place on the bench. There was only room for one, so she sat on the floor and motioned for her daughter to take my seat. Leaning toward me in a gesture of appreciation, the two bowed their heads and joined hands, never looking at the women who'd rejected them.

Wanting to make up for the rudeness of the others, I took out my camera and asked if I could I photograph them. They nodded, and I began to shoot—the mother's head on her beautiful daughter's lap, the protective arm on the shoulder, four eyes looking into me with weariness and wonder. I shot and shot, honoring them, thanking them, loving them. Our intimacy grew with every exposure.

Though I could not speak their language, kinship glimmered in their deep dark eyes. Through smiles and expressions, they offered me something of their essence, their inner light. And I gave back my own form of light, an adoring eye, a gaze wholly focused on the radiance I perceived. Whatever distance there was between us disappeared in those moments of complete attention. We were no longer separate parts; one existed where three had been before.

As a result of that connection, something shifted for the other women in the compartment as well, a subtle opening up, a moving toward. The women who had witnessed this encounter rearranged their bags and created more space for the mother and daughter. They opened up their lunch baskets and passed out *dosas* and fruit, handing portions to me and to the mother and daughter as well.

After our snack, I left the compartment and walked down the aisle to the train's open door, stretching out as far as I could into the hot, humid monsoon air. In a few minutes, the woman and her daughter appeared behind me and sat down on a bale of hay across from the door. They looked up at me smiling, and I sat down on the floor and took the mother's hand in mine. She leaned over and touched my face, stroking it like a mother would a child. The daughter reached out for my other hand. As the train rolled down the dusty track, we lingered there on the bale of hay, holding hands, rubbing palms.

The next stop was theirs. The women tugged on my arm, begging me with motions to come with them to their home. I was sorry I couldn't, but I had to be in Delhi the next day. As the train pulled away, I hung out the door waving until they were two tiny figures in the golden light.

Shortly after I returned to my seat, a porter arrived with a bottle of Campo Cola and a huge fresh orange. Gifts, he said, from the mother and her daughter. Though I thought no one in the cabin spoke English, one of the women said to me, "They were Muslim, you know. We do not associate. There is a war going on right now in the Golden Temple between Muslims and Hindus. A terrible massacre." It was then I realized what a social faux pas I had made, due to my ignorance of the culture. I nodded my head with a serious look on my face, taking it all in, reflecting on what unfolded, and ultimately, I was happy that I had made space for them, happy that we formed our little holy trinity on that bale of hay in the hallway. In this case, ignorance *was* bliss.

The threshold we're at right now is a precious one. The whole world is in our hands, and every one of us has the power to act consciously or not. If we do, what will change is us, what we'll save is ourselves—and what will happen in turn is a heightening of our joy and a deepening of our relationship to whatever we cherish.

LAUDS (SUNRISE)

I am an activity of the cosmos.
My life is a wild seed come to bloom in the soil of time.
I am intelligence ever-expanding
thought ushering forth from Divine Mind
A ray of light from the Original Source
I am the Great One taking shape in human form.
I am a chalice for the Holy Wine.

When my mother was living in upstate New York, she invited several friends over for a Christmas party. Since there was a fireplace in her newly rented apartment, she gathered lots of newspapers, put in some kindling, topped that off with some seasoned logs, and lit the fire just as the first guests began to arrive.

There was a great flurry of welcoming, shaking off snowboots, putting on slippers, hanging hats and coats on the rack. Lots of hugging, oohing and aahing over the tree, and carrying plates of food and fudge into the kitchen. Nobody noticed that the house was filling up with smoke until they all started coughing. By that time, the smoke was so thick they could hardly see each other. It was then my mother realized she had never opened the flue.

Our throats are like the flue. When we don't open them up, speak our truths, let out our feelings as they arise, the fire in our belly turns to smoke.

> *We have been socialized to respect fear more than our own needs for language and definition, and while we wait in silence for the final luxury of fearlessness, the weight of that silence will choke us...The transformation of silence into language and action is an act of self-revelation and that always seems fraught with danger. We fear the very visibility without which we also cannot truly live...and that visibility which makes us most vulnerable is that which is also the source of our greatest strength.*
> Audre Lorde

I call out like the rooster at sunrise
your name on my lips as I wake
what mystery is this I am part of
what is this force called divine?

They speak like you live in the heavens
though I feel you inside like a sun
burning away my illusions
till all that I am is your light.

My head is bowed daily in reverence
at my bedside I'm on bended knee
everywhere, every moment I feel you
there is nowhere to look you are not.

I cry at the wars we engage in,
the lives that are lost over greed
our actions are rooted in ignorance
fear is the seed of our sins.

I do not call out your name to save us
already you dwell in our midst
we are the vessels that hold you
through our hands does your love come to life.

I once visited my high school music teacher who was teaching a music
course at Catholic University in Washington, D.C. She had a guest in the class,
an Argentinian musicologist who had been studying with some medicine
women in the Andes. The musicologist asked for a volunteer to participate in
an exercise. A young man raised his hand and she had him lie down on the
carpet. She then held a pendulum over each of his chakras. The pendulum
swung in wide circles over his first three chakras and his sixth and crown, but
remained at a standstill over his heart and throat. They were emitting no vibrations whatsoever. She asked him to breathe deeply, then she held his feet and
sung a chant over him.

She asked five others of us to kneel at his head and by his arms and legs. Then she gave us a tone to sing, instructing us to sing it through clenched teeth so it would reverberate in our own bodies first. We did this for several minutes, singing the tone into his body, while she walked around and around us, shaking a rattle and chanting the tone.

Then she retested his chakras with the pendulum. At this point, the pendulum made complete circles over all his chakras, indicating that his energy was now flowing freely. When the exercise was over, the young man had tears in his eyes. He said that his girlfriend had left him recently and he had been full of sorrow and anxiety. His heart was breaking and he had no words to express his grief, so his heart and throat centers closed down.

The woman told him to start breathing consciously, and with the power of his breath, he could revitalize his own energy system. "You can breathe your way back to health," she said. "Just stop a few times during the day, close your eyes, and breathe love into your heart and your whole being. Your breath will open your centers and the flow of spirit will heal you."

The throat chakra is our will center. It is known in Hindu as the Vissudha, which means "purification." It is the place where the wisdom and feelings of our heart and lower chakras synthesize with the energies from above to be released as something new into the world. Its healthfulness is related to how honestly we express ourselves. If we lie, or refuse to speak authentically, we constrict its energy, violating the body and the spirit. If we express our truths fearlessly, open the flue fully, we increase the flow of energy throughout our entire being.

Song: (This is a love song where my body and spirit give thanks to each other)
My body, my temple, my palace,
My body, my vessel , my chalice
I thank you for being my home away from home
For giving me a chance to be on earth.

O Spirit, My wisdom, my wellspring,
My question, my answer, my knowing
With open arms and bended knee
I call you to my breast
Where you will find a holy place to rest.

PRIME (6:00 A.M.)

All praise to you my Love
All gratitude your way
All praise to you my Love
I offer you this day.

All praise to you my Light
For every breath I take
All praise to you my Light
For the dawn to which I wake.

We live on a tectonically unstable planet. The rose doesn't ask in a wind-storm, "What did I do to deserve this?" The forest doesn't look at the maple ripped apart by lightning and say "God has punished it for wrongdoing." We are the children of the Holy Mystery, born of the marriage of heaven and earth. Our bodies are made of stardust and clay, our spirits are as infinite as Creation Itself.

We are vulnerable and invincible, wise and wicked, generous and greedy. The line between good and evil runs from the temple to the toes of each of us. When evil occurs and drops us to our knees, all we can do is intensify our light, turn up our heat against the chill of the dark.

Do not think of God as a punishing force, as the creator of events that rob us of hope. Look instead inside yourself and ask what you can be to the ones cry-ing out, ask where to shine your light to overcome the shadow. The mysteries of life keep us in awe and protect us from arrogance—that is their gift to us, as the gift of an ending is a new beginning. In this human lifetime, evil haunts and humbles us day and night. Catastrophes confound us, paradox surrounds us, and there is nothing for us to do but give what we can give, withhold judg-ment, radiate kindness, and use every sorrow as a stepping stone to love.

God's handwriting is so bad sometimes
I can hardly make out the words on the page.
My pace is like a snail when I pen my questions
one by one, but the answers come
at roadrunner speed making me wonder
if a court reporter might be useful here.
I like it, though, that there's always a response
always that feeling I'm not alone
that somewhere in the deep dark down of me
is someone with a map whenever I am lost.

Revelation is an unveiling. It comes to the heart. When you truly hear, you will know. And when you say to another what you truly know, you will speak with the power of a prophet. Edward Brennan

Morning Prayers

This is heaven.
This cup of coffee, divine.
This air I am awash in,
sacred as the feather of an angel's wing.
This candle flame, Immanence Itself.
The stack of books, these poems and journals
The Word revealed anew.
This sound of silence,
The voice of the creators at it again
Earth and sky, particle and wave,
North and south, melting into One
fusing into future,
as I lie here in wonder
happy as a loon on a mountain lake.

How do you recognize a false prophet?
1. If when they say we, they don't mean everyone
2. If the story they tell doesn't inspire you to act for the common good
3. If they do not speak out when unity is disrupted

Song: I Am the River, You are the Flow

Do not complain,
your gifts are so many
you have breath and sight
and life all around
don't let yourself worry
or dwell on what's missing
for all that you need already abounds.

There is food for the hungry,
you need only to share it
all truth is revealed,
you need only to see
each soul I've created
contains all the heavens
I am there in your midst,
look around you, that's me.

Others may tell you
your sins keep us separate
they'll speak of the miles
between heaven and earth
but I tell you, my child,
there's no distance between us
I'm the light of your fire,
you're the sound of my breath.

And I hold you like sunshine
and bright colored flowers
I am one with you always,
I never let go
wherever you journey,
I journey beside you
for you are the river
and I am the flow.

TERCE (9:00 A.M.)

*How could we not be one
when the lines of your poem
fall like a bucket
into the well of my heart?*

I bought a statue of Buddha in Tijuana before heading to the east coast. With all my luggage in the trunk of my Honda, the only place I had to put him was in the passenger's seat. So I strapped him in and off we went. Being a gypsy at heart, I had driven across country a dozen times before, but never had a jaunt gone quite like this one.

Externally, everything looked much the same. Lonely, endless highways through the desert; steep, hairpin curves through the Rockies; quaking in the wake of massive diesel trucks; day after day of barrenness through Texas; lightning storms through the Midwest; endless construction through Pennsylvania, and dozens of pit stops along the way for food and coffee that never managed to flow through the body with any regularity.

After awhile, you know what to expect. The usual discomfort of sitting so long and eating wrong; the long stretches with nothing on the radio but right wing religion; the borderline panic attacks when there's no sign of life in the desert, or too much of it in the cities. Then of course, the fear of tornadoes in Kansas, of heights in Colorado, and armadillos in Louisiana. These are the common perils of the cross country trek.

But with Buddha at my side, everything changed. I don't know if it was me or Buddha, but for the first time, not a thing came up that caused me grief. No fear through the desert, in the mountains. No hassle from any trucker or roadside rowdy. No indigestion, no panic, no problems. And every minute behind the wheel, I was calm and collected in the presence of that little guy next to me.

What images we expose ourselves to, in our real lives and in our imagination, have a powerful impact on how we feel. Having that statue of Buddha beside me altered my experience on that road trip. It calmed me down, changed my way of feeling and thinking. It kept me mindful of his words, "We are what we think. All that we are arises with our thoughts. With our thoughts we make the world." I could not, in the presence of the master of mindfulness, absentmindedly drift into negative thinking. My thoughts stayed positive. My trip was a joy.

To Be List

Star in the sky of God
Kernel in the cornfield of God
Word in the encyclopedia of God
String in the orchestra of God
Trout in the stream of God
Window pane in the conservatory of God
Nanosecond in the light-year of God
Snowflake in the blizzard of God
Marshmallow in the campfire of God
Ink drop in the fountain pen of God
Sap in the maple tree of God
Ice crystal in the glacier of God
Grain of sand in the beach of God
Thread in the comforter of God
Decibel in the laugh of God
Blade of grass in the fairway of God
Hydrogen molecule in the sea of god
Consonant in the autobiography of God
Bulb in the greenhouse of God
Calorie in the coconut cream pie of God
Half-note in the symphony of God
Blank in the scrabble game of God
Pine needle in the forest of God
Bristle in the paintbrush of God
Diamond in the mine of God
Apple in the orchard of God
Grape in the Gewürztraminer of God
Feather in the wing of God
Viridian in the palette of God
Cell in the right brain of God.

To create is to make something whole from the pieces of our lives and, in the process, to become more whole ourselves. It is a healing act, a leave-taking from the chaos as we move from the choppy surface toward the stillness of the center. What was the last thing you created? What pieces were you putting together? Was it healing?

Into your hands I commend my failures,
my rash judgments, my criticisms,
my proneness for separation,
my harsh opinions.
Into the bowl of your cosmic lap
I heave my ten thousand undigested sorrows,
my tempests of thoughtlessness,
my ramblings of misery, chaos, loneliness.

Lies, lies, all of them!

Me falling into this featherbed of forgetfulness:
O, what a sight!
Remove all mirrors when I flail like this,
when I become a lost one
wandering in the dark.

Imagine that when we're born, each one of us comes to earth with the radiance of, say, a hundred watt bulb. That's our natural state—100 watts. As we go through life, our job is to maintain that brightness, and even improve it if we can. What dims it, we learn through experience, is negativity, anger, resentments, regrets. What brightens it is harmony, balance, joy.

If you consider the people you encounter on a regular basis and reflect a little on their energy level, you could probably bring to mind a few who fit the 100 watt category, and others who are in the 50-60 watt vicinity. And you probably encounter 10 watt people every once in a while, though chances are you don't linger long. It's the 100 watt-ers that keep your attention. These are people who don't complain, who don't say negative things about themselves or others, who are the first to offer help and the ones who stay until the work is done.

Hundred watt-ers laugh a lot, they draw people in like bears to honey. They're the ones you wish you were more like. And now, you can choose to become one, if you want. All it takes is a little practice. First, you must become an observer to your own thoughts and words, so you are conscious of your thoughts and the words that you speak. Second, you must speak as if your words were materializing into your very life. This means no self-deprecating remarks and no negative comments about others. In other words, you must actually *love* yourself and love others *as* yourself.

If we operate from this premise, than we have a good chance of keeping our light bright. If we speak positively, think reverently, then we maintain our original state of grace. If we enter into a meeting imagining that every person there is a peer, then our encounters will begin to change. Once we start noticing our thoughts, becoming aware of their power, letting go of judgments, resistance, opposition, then we experience a more radiant energy. As we think, so shall it be. As we speak, so shall we create.

The rule that covers everything is: How you are with others, expect that back. Rumi

SEXT (NOON)

As others have calmed me on turbulent nights
as they've led me to shelters away from the storm
may the love of my heart be like dawn to their darkness
may the mirror of my eyes let them see their own light.

Our body and brain are the physical manifestation of our immaterial mind. The mind is like the symphony, and the body and brain are the instruments and players. Every second a massive information exchange is occurring in the body and each system has its own unique tone—a signature tune. These tunes rise and fall, wax and wane, bind and unbind, according to Dr. Candace Pert who writes: *"If we could hear this body music with our ears, the sum of the sounds would be the music we call emotions."*

Our raw emotions are striving to be expressed in the body. They're always moving up and down the chakras and the spinal cord, carrying information on a cellular level, communicating through a psychosomatic network with every system in our body, and seeking a final release and integration through the brain. They're like seedlings burrowing through the soil in search of the sun. If they are stunted in their journey, denied expression, there is no flow, no growth.

Releasing our emotions is part of the process of unmanifest consciousness becoming manifest. It's through the expression of our emotions that we, as incarnate versions of the Divine, allow the Beloved to flow through us and become present in our world.

The alienation we feel is not about distance from God, but about our estrangement from creation which was, and continues to be, God's first revelation to humanity. Diarmuid O'Murchu

NONE (3:00 PM)

Finding Yourself on Sacred Ground

There is nowhere else to find yourself,
since all ground is sacred,
nowhere to kneel that before you
the Holy One is not in sight.

If the noise of the city makes you scream
and stuff cotton in your ears
it does not mean the One Who Made You
is faraway.

It means your soul needs quiet now:
the canopy of an oak tree,
the silence of a forest,
the calm of the sunset on a canyon ridge.

The ground is holy wherever you stand
the Windmaker never moves out of sight.
To find that One, turn just slightly to the left,
ready yourself for wonder,
and open your eyes.

In 1967, when I was eighteen, I entered a convent. After two years, I was dismissed for "lack of a religious disposition." The news that I had to leave came suddenly; one night, without warning, my parents appeared to take me home. I had no chance to say good-bye to the friends I was leaving behind, and was told by my Superior as she ushered me through the basement corridors, "We don't want you communicating with anyone here. The sisters will keep you in their prayers."

I moved to California from New York shortly thereafter. Nine months later, as the birthday of my best friend in the Novitiate was approaching, I decided to make her a birthday present. I would create an album of photographs and quotations that might convey, in the language of images, all that I wished I could say to her. Since mail was censored by the order's superiors, I tried to keep the album as impersonal as possible. No card. No letter. No notes on the page other than quotations from authors we'd loved, songs we'd sung together, prayers and poems we'd passed back and forth. The photographs had to do most of the work. In their silent language, they had to reveal me, speak the words I couldn't say, carry the weight of my tangled feelings, my failed attempts to get past the pain.

With a Kodak Instamatic in hand, I went out in search of pictures to portray my struggle to reassemble my life, to regain my footing and rekindle my joy. I rummaged for images that would *be* the words I wanted to speak, that could whisper my voice in every color and shade of gray.

I went to the mountains and the desert, the ocean and forests. I found myself reflected in parched desert floors, redwood saplings, homeless park dwellers. I photographed footsteps dissolving in the tide, my body against a twelve-foot cross, my shadow in front of a locked church door. Images of crashing waves and toppled sand castles, friends huddled on a moonlit beach, a woman alone strumming a guitar, birds soaring into golden sunsets—each reflected something I felt but could not say, a metaphor for a sentiment I could not share.

As the photos were developed, I studied each one, looking for the emotions they contained—finding strength in one, fear in another, loneliness and joy and conviction in others. Everything I had experienced since I left the Motherhouse was captured in those prints—the rejection that seemed to have come from God, the loss of my community, the loneliness for my friends, the fear of what was to come, the doubt about my own worth, the disappointment that I could not have the life I felt called to, the anger at being dismissed without a chance to defend myself.

In my quest for photographs that would tell my story, I revealed myself to myself in a new way. Photography pushed me to understand each feeling in order to portray it. Every detail mattered immensely. The light mattered, the shadows mattered, the mood and tone and contrast mattered. There was nothing else on the page—only one image after another saying:

Dear Lois,

Here I am. Here is how I'm doing. This is what I'm thinking. This page is my loss. This page is the joy I am trying to hold onto. Here is the fragment of my faith that remains. Here is my long, lonely howl in the night.

Making that album was a healing ritual from beginning to end. It gave me a new way to let grief out—to see it, experience it, understand it. In the process, my sorrow became less a malignancy I was bent on destroying and more a companion I was seeking to befriend. As I glued each photograph onto the page, I was touched by its power, in awe of its ability to give voice to my silence, shed light on my darkness.

I almost didn't matter, by the time it was done, if the book made it to Lois after all. It had done far more work than I'd ever imagined, helping me to know my feelings, then express and release them. As it turned out, when the book arrived, Lois was summoned by the Novice Director who had her read the book in her presence. Page by page, Lois studied the pictures, read the quotations, and entered the world between my lines. In that process, we connected across three thousand miles and she knew what a long, long way I was from home.

In the course of manifesting what we hold within, transforming spirit and ideas into matter and language, we experience the delight of creation. As we give form to Spirit, so are we informed and healed by it. As we express the Divine through our creative work, so do we experience the Divine within. What exists in the world that wouldn't be here if you weren't?

VESPERS (SUNSET)

O Mother, O Source, O Giver of Life
I bow to you, I kiss your fingers,
I lift my arms in praise and joy.
Alleluia! I am born and born again
all the days of my life.

I was once staying at a Gandhian ashram when the community came to-gether to build a new barn. Eighty people gathered at the river bed, which was about a quarter of a mile away from the building site. They formed a long line from the stream, up a hill, through a meadow and to the site of the new barn. It was monsoon season, the temperature was 104 degrees and the air was thick with humidity.

Our job was to pass tin bowls of sand, stones and water from the stream to the building site. From one person to the other, hand to hand, the bowls were passed along the snaking line. Hour after hour went by and no one com-plained. By noon, I was soaking wet and losing steam. At one point, I scanned the landscape for signs of relief, finding two tractors in a nearby meadow and two empty carts on the side of the road. Moments later, a group of ashram kids passed by leading a team of oxen to the river. I thought it was ridiculous that all this people power was being used for something that oxen, tractors and wooden carts could do.

"This is stupid!" I shouted to Nayan Bala, an English-speaking woman from Delhi who stood next to me in line. "We've got 80 people here wasting a whole morning in this heat, when we could just hook up the carts to those trac-tors and oxen and let them do the work in half the time. Don't you know time is money?"

I knew, even as those final words tumbled out of my mouth, that every one of them was a mistake, but they were traveling too fast to stop. Nayan Bala put her bowl down and walked over to my side. Gently, she put her hand on my sweaty arm and whispered in my ear, "These people are proud to be building this barn with their own hands. One day they will bring their children and grandchildren here and tell them how they helped build it, rock by rock. They are all proud to be here. You wouldn't want to take that from them would you?"

I was too humbled and ashamed to say anything more, but Nayan Bala gave me the gift of a lifetime that day. She brought her East to my West, her peaceful- ness to my anger, and in that loving moment I learned a lesson I'll never forget.

We are penetrating and being penetrated by an archetypal Ground of Being in an effort to bring into consciousness whatever it can of the vast unknown.
                                                                    Marion Woodman

Magdalene's Diary

He is not so gentle as they say or think—
a thundercloud on some nights,
a hurricane of sorrow on others.
No one sees this private man as I see him
his hands big as the world
clenched in madness one moment,
folded in prayer the next.

At night it is I who must calm him down
remove his robe, kiss his face
wrap my arms round his burdened back,
rub his heavy laden shoulders with healing balm.

He needs me as the others need him
which causes fury in a few of them.
Peter's rage and jealousy has frightened me
more than once
though I don't share that with Yeshua—
he has enough problems with them
without adding that to his list.

They call him Master,
though he asks them only to master themselves,
to make of their lives what he is making of his.

What anger he feels
when they won't take their power
saying he is the Master, his gifts are unique

Over and over he repeats the same thing:
Anything I have done, you can do, and more.
He calls them to manhood
yet they refuse to grow up
and though I know his thoughts as I know my own
they will not listen when I speak his truth.
I bear the sorrows of my beloved each night,
as I offer him bread and a cup of wine.
Into my lungs I breathe his pain,
out of my mouth, I send forth my love.

His tears fall like blood
from a heart broken open
He thrashes in his sleep
like a boat in a storm.

Though separate we are one,
our spirits undivided,
he is the dawn of my every day
and I am his northern star.

Deep dialogue is essential to creative thinking because it is a tool for helping us discover what we value and why. As soon as you speak of your values, your visions, your fears, my mind begins a search to discover its own beliefs in the matter. We are hardwired to compare and contrast, to scan for differences and similarities, to take in and synthesize and evolve ourselves forward. We define ourselves through problems, which are statements of contrast, not absolutes. And in order to arrive at these statements of contrast, we need to hear each other's stories.

They are the grist for our mills. Your deep telling feeds my deep knowing. Or as the French poet Paul Valéry expressed it: *Nothing is more 'original,' nothing more 'oneself,' than to feed on others. But one has to digest them. A lion is made of assimilated sheep.* The truths we cling to are based on the stories we've been told, and they are altered and enlivened by the stories we continue to hear. We take something in, we digest it, we decide what to keep and what to let go of. Sometimes we change our thinking. Sometimes we don't.

COMPLINE (9:00 P.M.)

Prayer for Kind Speaking

Be my speaking, You, the Word
that tells no bitter lie
shape my lips in such a way
that only You get by

Take away my anger
cast out all my need to blame
let my words be comforting,
a balm to someone's pain.

Let me not forget the power
of words to soothe the soul,
Let my stories be a fire
to lost ones in the cold.

Be my words, come flood my mind
come drench my every cell,
till every thought beneath my speaking
rises up from You as well.

It's not easy these days, making time for our creative work. Voices call us from everywhere demanding our attention, our energy. And many of us, some-where along the line, got the message that making art is self-indulgent, so we relegate it to the bottom of our list. It becomes the thing we get to when the laundry is done, the bills are paid, the groceries bought and put away, the e-mail is answered.

We get so caught up in the flurry of our lives that we forget the essential thing about art—that the act of creating is a healing gesture, as sacred as prayer, as essential to the spirit as food is to the body. Our creative work reveals us to ourselves, allows us to transform our experience and imagination into forms that sing back to us in a language of symbol who we are, what we are becoming, what we have loved and feared. This is the alchemy of creation: that as I attempt to transmute a feeling or thought into an artistic form that can be experienced by another, I myself am added to, changed in the process.

As we center ourselves in the act of creating, attune to our inner voice, a shift occurs in our consciousness, allowing for the birth of something new. Our attention is no longer on time and demands and errands. It is caught up in the extraordinary metamorphosis of one thing into another. What begins as cocoon emerges a butterfly. What once was sorrow may now be a song.

As I am changed by the art that passes through me in the process of becoming, so am I changed by the creations of others. I am moved, in some way, by every image I encounter, as I am moved by music, poetry, plays, and novels. I am healed by the creations of others every day, conscious of the obstacles that each artist faced in the process of birthing them, and aware that if they did it, so can I; and if I do it, so can you.

For it is the same with all of us—we have our fears, our doubts, our cultures that negate the work of the spirit. And yet we continue on, journeying inward to find what is there that seeks release and offers comfort. Over and over, we transmute one thing into another, turning tragedies and triumphs into powerful images, colorful landscapes, illuminating poems. We conjure these images in our private hours and offer them to the whole like food for the soul, a wrap against the cold.

The call to create is a calling like no other, a voice within that howls for expression, the shadow longing to merge with the Light. It is an act of faith to respond to this voice, to give it our time; and in return we are blessed with work that has light and life of its own. One photograph can spark a revolution, thaw a frozen heart, inspire another's masterpiece.

Art that emerges from our inward journeys is a tale-telling mirror that collapses time and expands dimension. Our creations contain the past and the future, the known and the unknown, the breath of spirit and the heft of matter. As we respond to the world we are part of, what we create adds to its essence, changes its shape, heals its wounds. No matter what the medium, art reveals us to ourselves and raises the level of human consciousness. Art is a mirror not only to the soul of the artist, but to the whole of civilization that celebrates its creation.

Simone Weil once wrote: "The work of art which I do not make, none other will ever make it." We, as creators, hold in our bones the lessons of history, paths to the future, glimpses of a world yet to come. The lines that we draw are lifelines, lines that connect, lines that sketch the contours of the future we're creating.

It is up to us—those who feel the tug of the inner voice—to create the world we want to be a part of, to utter the words we want to inspire us.

If, through our images, we can reveal the heart of humankind, shine a light on what is precious and holy in ourselves and others, then let us find that in our midst and capture it in our work. Let us not wait for the heroic, conspicuous gestures, but rather look more carefully for those small, daily kindnesses, those rituals of bonding and sharing that show us as people revering life, revering each other. Our sensibilities are assaulted on a daily basis by a press consumed with fear and destruction. Heartbreaking photos of a world run amok wash over our days, invade our dreams. The shadow of humanity makes the news, while the light goes unnoticed, the good unrevealed.

May we, as image makers, shapers of the culture, set our sights on things we value, rituals we engage in that heal and serve. May our images honor the ordinary endeavors of common people, and may they make their way to the eyes of the weary—light to the dark, fire to the chill.

There are a lot of things we don't have in life, but time is not one of them. Time is all we have. One lifetime under this name to produce a body of work that says, "This is how I saw the world."

Each of us is here to express our potential, manifest that *something* that's unique to us. None of us is aiming for triteness, in pursuit of the shallow. It's greatness we're after—and not some hollow applause coming from somewhere beyond us, but the deep down thrill of knowing we went all out, put our soul into something, created a life or a piece of art that sparked something new, had an impact, could be of use.

I want my fire to blaze, to rage up and light some piece of night that someone's shivering into. I want my life, my work to sizzle with passion, to ignite ideas and laughter and wonder and kindness, to spread hope like wildfire through these times of darkness. We're a culture in big trouble, making big mistakes, and everyone knows it. We need help, and it's the arts that can help us,

84

because it is our spirit that is wounded, and that's where art goes. That's where it performs its healing magic.

You can build a temple in the space between your eyes.

I once noticed in the credits to a film that someone had a job called "fly wrangler." There was a scene where a body had been dead a long time and there were hundreds of flies swarming around. The fly wrangler had to see to it that those flies behaved well and did their part. As you begin to pay attention to your thoughts and words, you're going to start noticing others' speaking as well, and you can take on the role of "conversation wrangler."

If you're with someone or a group of people who are being critical or negative, you can wrangle that conversation right around to something positive. Think of it as a creative challenge. How can you kindly, compassionately redirect the energy toward the light? How can you reframe the issue so people can focus on what they want, instead of what they don't want?

If I put my cheek against the earth's body, I feel the pulse of God.
                                                            Meister Eckhart

The apostle Philip says to Jesus, "I do see you, but I want to see God." And Jesus responds, "Whoever sees anything at all is looking into the eyes of the Only One Who Is." We are evolving toward this consciousness, but it is a rigorous climb, entrenched as we are in old ways of thinking. The very culture that has shaped us is the culture we must now transcend, and we will do that by co-creating it consciously day by day. Our neighborhoods, our cities, our churches, our workplaces looks like they look because we co-create them. They are made of our energy, our commitments, our ideas and creations. They are what they are because of what we have done or failed to do.

I can imagine that people looking back on our world from a hundred years in the future will be horrified that we allowed 40,000 children a day to die from hunger when there was plenty of food to go around. That we poisoned our rivers, destroyed our forests, considered war a viable option. I can imagine them with saddened faces, poring over documents of our devastating history, trying to understand the suicide of children, the stoning of women, the obesity of one nation and the starvation of another. Why we spent more on smart bombs than smart children. Why we killed people to show people that killing people is wrong. Why so many billions of dollars were spent on drugs, plastic surgeries, prisons, and weapons, when just a few of those billions could have met the basic needs of every person on the planet. We are all involved in one of the greatest mysteries on earth: *why don't we care for each other?*

Prophets play a part in the whole history of a nation, whether in confraternities or singly as influential persons. At times the prophet may be powerful enough to reprove a king or direct national policy; at other times s/he may be in lonely opposition and her message takes the form of a tissue of menaces and reproaches against the ruling powers. Jerusalem Bible

Every human being is like a leaf on a tree, receiving sunlight and rain and converting these into food for itself. This process in nature is called photosynthesis. The magic ingredient is chlorophyll. In humans, it is called *infosynthesis*, and the magic ingredient is our imagination.

We convert what comes our way into stories, into youtube movies, into text messages, books, and facebook pages. We are social turbines converting the winds of change into power for the multitudes. Part of what makes us human is our ability to share our experience—to make it through the desert and leave behind a journal that's a guidebook for others. This is our nature. We share what we notice to help the ones who are behind us. The pioneers leave word of the shortcuts and dangers.

We become prophetic when we recognize where justice is absent and strive to correct it. We absorb knowledge and convert it to wisdom when we apply it for the betterment of all. Knowledge by itself is information. Knowledge mixed with compassion turns into prophetic action. Facts become transformed into essays, sermons, letters to the editor, poems and plays. Information comes to life in the process of infosynthesis. It is transmuted into intelligence and inspired action.

We do this on a small scale with our families, but as we grow in consciousness, more of the world comes into our view. The prophets among us are in service to the many. They have a worldview. They commit themselves to justice. They are a stand for unity. They are the yang to the mystics' yin. If you watched them for a week, you could see their dedication. You would see the hours they devote, the energy they contribute to peace on the planet. This is evolutionary creativity: when we engage in the transformation of thoughts into language, language into practice, and when the practices of our lives encourage, sustain and energize others. This is prophetic work. We are not predicting the future. We are giving birth to it, co-creating it in consort with the Great Mystery. We bring our consciousness to the table and it meets with the unknown cosmic forces. This is the creative dance of a lifetime. This is truly "dancing with the stars."

Where does revelation come from these days? Not burning bushes. Not voices in the sky asking you to kill your son. Not snakes in the desert. Nor snakes in the garden. Revelation comes quietly, in times of stillness, when one ponders how to be of use. Revelation comes at the intersection of compassion and the daily news. Revelation rises up in response to injustice—as it rose up in Moses, in Jesus, in Harriet Tubman, Mahatma Gandhi, Rosa Parks, Martin Luther King, Jr., Mother Teresa, and the ones who've stood up and spoken out for the benefit of others.

Revelation is in the air we breathe. It has never changed. It never will. It is always the same: *Take care of each other. I am with you and in you.*

The heart is a sophisticated information processing center with its own nervous system. It has the ability to sense, learn, remember, and make functional decisions independent of the brain. It sends messages to the brain and the rest of the body in four different languages—neurological, bio-physical, hormonal, and electrical. Research from the Institute of Heart Math in northern California shows that by simply shifting our heart's rhythmic beating patterns from chaotic to coherent we can produce profound and beneficial changes in the brain. These changes open the brain up so we can see the big picture and build new neural pathways that allow us to more easily experience positive emotions.

With the power of our own consciousness, we can cause a change in the rate of our heartbeat and create new pathways in the brain that lead to expanded imagination, evolutionary creativity, and more visionary solutions.

The heart's energy field is coupled with a subtle energetic field of ambient intelligence which is limitless and perpetually accessible. Love is dancing with wisdom all day long. Real learning, for the most part, is an unconscious process. It happens when we are most present—body, mind, and spirit—to what is before us.

If we overwhelm ourselves with too much information, our brain's synthesizing functions exhaust themselves trying to keep up. The challenge is not to overload the brain with data, but to open the channels for information to drift down into the heart. The goal is to embody the wisdom of the cosmos, to be aware that our consciousness is one with the ever expanding universe. Our bodymind is a manifestation of nature's quintessential being.

CHAPTER FOUR THURSDAY

Statistically, at every degree of evolution, we find evil always and everywhere. This is relentlessly imposed by the play of large numbers at the heart of a multitude undergoing organization. The human epic resembles nothing so much as a way of the cross. Teilhard de Chardin (1881-1955)

THE MYSTERY OF EVIL

A friend once said to me, after the publication of my last book, "I'd like to read a book about your struggles, your questions, and how you're wrestling with them. It's great to know what you know, but I'm more interested in what you *want* to know, what you *don't* know." It's an interesting idea for an author to ponder: writing a book about what one doesn't know—and this is not that book, but it may be this chapter.

To skip the subject of evil in any book on spirituality would be a huge oversight. And yet, there's nothing I struggle with more, nothing I know less about than the nature of evil. It is everywhere around us, advancing as exponentially as we appear to be advancing in intelligence. It is the shadow to our light, and therefore I suspect, it will always be with us. But I am hopeful, as I believe along with Helen Keller that "although the world is full of suffering, it is full also of the overcoming of it."

Our world was turned upside down on September 11, 2001, and the confounding mystery of evil continues to torture us as terrorism grows like a tumor in the heart of our collective body. We try to wage a war against it, but that perpetuates the evil. We cannot solve today's challenges with yesterday's cannons. We cannot continue to imagine that war is a solution to any crisis. This is not the Middle Ages. This is the time in history when humans have become aware of ourselves as *agents* of evolution. It is not happening *to* us, but *through* us. It is not a higher caliber of weaponry that will bring about our success, but a higher caliber of consciousness.

We cannot look behind us for answers. They do not live there. We must *imagine* ourselves forward, envision the world we want to create, and feel the new reality in every cell of our beings in order to bring it about—for it is our feelings, our passions and compassion, that will propel us toward the future we desire. The question is not *what is wrong and how can we fix it?* The question is *what does the world we want to live in look like?*

Until we get a picture of it in our minds, we cannot manifest it. If we see it fully, imagine it fearlessly, hold to it wholeheartedly, despite criticism or opposition from others, then we create the possibility for its being. We become the vessels for its expression, and through us the new will arrive. Just like the fulfillment of every dream you've ever made come true. You imagine it, you feel it happening long before it ever happens, you save for it, invest in it, give your heart to it, and one day…you enter into it.

Joseph Campbell was a modern day prophet dedicated to throwing new light on old subjects. As a story-teller and mythologist, he offered images to advance our spiritual and cultural maturity, encouraging us to see how influenced we are by ancient myths and to begin to unfold new ones that reflect our contemporary challenges. In *Myths to Live By*, he writes:

> We are the children of this beautiful planet. We were not delivered into it by some god, but have come forth from it. We are its eyes and mind, its seeing and its thinking. And the earth, together with its sun, came forth, we are told, from a nebula; and that nebula, in turn, from space. No wonder then, if its laws and our laws are the same. Likewise our depths are the depths of space…We can no longer hold our loves at home and project our aggressions elsewhere; for on this spaceship Earth there is no 'elsewhere' any more. And no mythology that continues to speak or to teach of 'elsewheres' and 'outsiders' meets the requirement of this hour.

The requirement of this hour is an awareness of our oneness. It is openness to a new story that will surface in our lives, our families, and our communities when we come together and speak from our hearts. It is a willingness to see ourselves as co-creators of the world we are immersed in, and to shape the world that we want to leave our children and grandchildren.

This is what we do to counter evil. We enact its opposite into the world as creatively and vigorously as we can. For individuals dedicated to shifting the tides of global consciousness, to co-creating a higher order of planetary priorities, it is particularly important to convene with others, to unfold visions in the presence of others, to invite the unfolding of theirs, for it is out of our collective imagining that the new ways will be revealed to and through us.

And because we are dealing with an entirely new worldview, with the creation of a new myth, based not on separation and a fall from grace, but on oneness and ascendancy into our true potential, the revelations of our collective wisdom will take some time to supersede the old myths. They will meet with opposition, cynicism, and a wild clamoring against change. Since so many are profiting from things as they are, and since we collectively fear letting go of the known, the forerunners of change will be addressing minds that are closed and frightened. And this is the great challenge for any emergent prophet or visionary—to know that one's ideas will be criticized and resisted, and yet to dare to speak, knowing that these thoughts are the only building blocks we have to a new and safer world.

MATINS (MIDNIGHT)

I will not leave you comfortless,
I will not leave you alone
I am the air you breathe in
I'm the light of every star and every dawn.

The people of Israel are inside me.
Moab and the Assyrians roam through my deserts.
A slave bends over in tears,
my whip cuts red lines into his back.
Lot sleeps with his daughter in my loins,
their children taste like gall on my lips.
God calls to Moses from a bush
To Abraham, he speaks through an angel
Part the sea, he cries to one.
Kill your son, he orders the other.

What language does the Holy One speak?
Where must I go to hear it?
Is the bush burning in Brooklyn and Baghdad?
Are the angels getting orders in Burundi?

On a walk the other day, I came across two boys fighting in the front yard.
One was on top of the other, twisting the arm of the underdog, yelling "Say it!
Say it!" I thought he meant "Say UNCLE!"—a phrase we used to make our
childhood enemies utter as a signal of defeat.

As I got closer to the battlefield, I realized I was wrong. He wasn't waiting for
the word "uncle" at all. Just as I passed them, the younger one shouted out,
"OK, OK, I love you!" That was the phrase that ended the battle. Once he said
that, he was let up and the two bolted into the side yard chasing each other
and whooping it up. Should all wars end so easily.

I am Waiting
(after Lawrence Ferlinghetti)

I am waiting
for the redwoods to pick up their roots
and leave the forest.

I am waiting for the elders
to jump out of their wheelchairs
and cha cha down the long lonely hallway.

I am waiting for every 9th grader in America
to board a school bus bound for Washington,
camp out for a week on the floors of Congress
and talk some sense into elected leaders.

I'm waiting for the thunder
to shake us from our sleep
for the tropical winds to melt the frozen parts
inside us and warm us up
to the lovely sight
of the one walking toward us.

I'm waiting for a new dawn to wake up into
where women in Darfur are writing books
women in Tehran are teaching the tango
women in Gaza City and Jerusalem are dismantling walls
brick by brick

I'm waiting for the end of the red, white and blues,
the end of commercialism, consumerism, capitalism

I'm waiting for the future to enter into me,
the past to drain out of me,
for evolution to rip through me like a tornado

sucking into its funnel
every judging tendency
every old notion that's had its day
and is due to retire.

I'm waiting for fundamentalism to die
so freedom can live
for churches and temples and mosques
to be places of laughter
where the hungry are fed,
the sick are healed,
the elders are cared for.

I'm waiting for people to
believe in the words
whatever I have done in the name of the Creator
you can do as well, and even more.

I'm waiting for the children to teach us,
the trees to save us, the oceans to sail us
into truer horizons
where we can see—
in spite of this darkness—
from the eye of the storm
the Holy One watches.

LAUDS (SUNRISE)

The mysteries I wake up to are mighty
The dark is always on its way
Let me use this daylight wisely
Let me cast my love to those who sit in fear.

Though many years had gone by, I wasn't able to shake the grief I felt at being dismissed from the convent. I was still bound somehow, still resentful, still blaming the community for banishing me from the one life that felt right for me. I could not find the path of my heart because my heart was locked up, and I could not unlock it on my own.

It was in 1991, twenty-two years after my dismissal, that I called the sister who was Provincial Director when it happened. I asked if she would just sit with me while I told her the story of what happened and how it felt. That was all I wanted, a witness from the community. She agreed and we set a date. When I arrived at her convent, we went out to the screened-in porch and sat down, knee to knee across from each other.

"I'm going to start when I was twelve, when I first decided to be a nun," I said. "I'll probably cry through the whole story, but I just want you to listen from the beginning to the end, alright?" She nodded. For the next hour, I drained out all my feelings and memories about the whole incident. I was honest about my broken heart, my shattered faith, my inability to find another path for myself while I was harboring all this sorrow and resentment. "I just want to let it go, Sister. I want to let it go and I need your help," I sobbed. "Can you help me get free of this?"

She took my hands in hers and said, "Sister, will you forgive me personally for the part I played in this deep and terrible pain of yours?" I shook my head yes. "And will you forgive the community for the pain we caused you and for the mistakes we made in dealing with you while you were with us?"

"Yes, Sister, I forgive the community," I said, and with that forgiveness came the release, the freedom I needed to go on with my life and find the path that was calling me. With that forgiveness came a surge of energy, a rush of tenderness I hadn't felt in twenty years. It opened me up, unlocked my heart. It was a step into freedom I couldn't make while I was clinging to my pain and anger.

Only after I forgave could I understand there was nothing to forgive. They did not cause me pain. They just did what they did. Pain was my response to it. Pain was me holding onto it. Pain was me refusing to accept the life before me. Once I released it, I could bless that time I had. I could see that two years in the Novitiate was all I needed there to establish my footings in a faith I was meant to live out more publicly. I was like a young eagle in a nest, peering over the edge, afraid to fly. And they nudged me out so I could soar. And so I am.

Yahweh's Lament

I look out and see you falling
your bodies and spirits are weary
for you have deprived them of silence
to the soul you have offered no bread.

Breath have I given you, by breath do I live in you
yet you take little notice, and offer no thanks
All that you want will be spread before you
when your mind awakens, and you sing out in joy.

Chaos is what you make of your days
disorder is rampant, injustice prevails
That you care for each other as you care for yourself
is my one request, yet what do you do?
You withhold your love from those who need you
you keep for yourselves the treasures you find.

Daily do I wake you, yet you sleep through your hours
thinking the thoughts of the feeble and weak.
Afraid of your shadow you run like a rabbit,
hide like a child in fear of the night.
How long will you take to do your part
to tend to the sick, bring hope to the poor?

Effortless is my way, yet you struggle and curse,
the mountains you face you have made,
the drought in this desert comes from your thoughts,
with your words do you carve out your days.

The way calls for diligence, not for tears
the morning sky sings praise to the sun
the dewdrops laugh, the gardenias giggle
yet you mutter and complain all day long.

*Hope is not the conviction that something will turn out well, but the certainty
that something makes sense, regardless of how it turns out.* Vaclav Havel

There is a truth within me. It's mine, because I've learned it through living. I did not inherit it. Perhaps it will resonate with a truth that it is in you and perhaps that resonance will lift you up, carry you forward. That is the reason I write these things. Not to say there is something I know that you should know too—as if there is an objective truth outside of us, the knowing of which will save us both.

I hold to the possibility that the only real truth is the pulsing light inside us. When you share yours with me, or I with you, the lights collide and fuse and everything in the vicinity of that vivifying force is touched and changed by the grace it carries.

The true prophets of this time are the ones who are not just imagining, not just hoping for and waiting for the new dispensation to arrive, but actively bringing it into existence. They are stepping out of the old roles, abandoning what does not serve the common good. Rising above popular opinion, social conditioning, conformist behavior, prophets of today are daring to speak the unspeakable, as Copernicus did, as Galileo did, as the mystics and poets and scientists throughout the ages did, guiding us into fuller awareness, deeper imagining. To bring anything into existence, to be a creator of circumstances, we have to imagine the new, then speak the new, then usher it into reality with the fierce force of our belief in it.

There are hundreds of books that have been written but not published because the writers imagined them well enough, wrote them well enough, but failed to believe in them enough to propel them into reality. If our founding fathers did not have faith in their words, if they were not fervent in their beliefs about a more perfect union, they could not have succeeded in shaping the contours of these United States.

And so with us, to bring about a world of unity, a planetary community, we must begin to imagine it, speak it, and believe it into existence. To end war, we must begin to say war is obsolete, and it is time to ban it, just as we banned slavery, child labor, witch-burning. To protect the planet or the poor, we must begin to say—convincingly and collectively—that corporations can profit as they wish, but not at the expense of the environment, of human rights, and of the communities in which they do business. This is not a revolution against something, it is an evolution toward something... toward a better quality of life for the whole human family.

You are alive at this point in history because on some level you chose to be. You came here to be of use, to add your creative genius to the mix, to make meaning of your human adventures and pass that meaning along to others who are seeking it. It is not some accident that you are alive. You are here to help. What is it you would fix if you had a magic wand? What would you heal if you could heal whatever you touched? Think of what would bring you joy if you could work miracles, and let your imagination go. This is what will lead you to the work you're meant to do and the place you're meant to be. All miracles start with a step in one direction. Jesus had to *get* himself to the wedding feast at Cana.

I tell you, just as you did not do it to one of the least of these, you did not do it to me. Matthew 25:43

Psalm for the Returning Light

As the darkness longs for break of day
so do we cry out for your light
Can you hear our howls in the night,
feel the trembling in our voices as we cry?

We bleat like lambs in the moors
thirsty, with no drink but our tears
We stumble on the path, tired and longing
our ears await the sound of your steps.

Our eyes stay open day and night
we look to the east and to the west
In the darkness our memory is fading
our kindness is turning to hate.

Grief and misery surround us
violence is pounding at the door
The light in our hearts is flickering
rivers of tears overflow.

Come lift us into your bosom
on your sturdy thighs let us rest
O Light shine down on our darkness
Let us feel again the warmth of your love.

If you do not tend to one another, who is there to tend you? Whoever would tend me, he should tend the sick. Buddha

I had my eyes examined today and the optician suggested artificial tears if my eyes were dry. "Artificial tears?" I cried in amazement. "Who in the world would need artificial tears? I cry at the drop of a hat. All I have to do is turn on CNN. Read the local newspaper. Watch the News at 11. There's enough tragedy going on to keep anyone crying all day long." We're at an all time low in national *joie de vivre*. It hurts to watch Congress. It's an outrage what's happening on Wall Street. Our trust is plummeting—in government, education, the military, health care. Our number one cause of death is heart disease, because our hearts are breaking all over the place. We seem to be in that breakdown mode that immediately precedes a breakthrough, and while we are ushering in a future that we can believe in, we are simultaneously mourning the death of what we once held true. What *is* the American Dream anyway? Is there such a thing anymore?

I had dinner at the home of an affluent friend the other night, and even though he's not worried for himself financially, he's concerned about the country his grandkids are inheriting. "It's the first time in history we are not passing down the promise of a better life to our kids. My parents had a better life than their parents. I have a better life than my parents. But I can't be sure that my children and grandchildren will have a better life than I do."

We're midwives and mourners, shifting constantly from hope to horror, delight to outrage. All around us we see evil, and all around us we see the constant transcending of it. We are evolving into people who can live in the in-between, who know there are mysteries greater than our ability to comprehend. One of the greatest gifts the Catholic Church ever gave me was the ability to be in awe, to dwell in mystery. I know adoration. I cherish my ability to adore. I wake up adoring life, adoring earth, adoring dawn and the sound of the birds… and I know that all day long I'll encounter things that are awry, things that I cannot set right.

The ability to dwell in mystery, to be comfortable in that space between the dissolution of old ideas and the emergence of the new is a required skill these days. We need to be courageous and humble enough to suspend our beliefs long enough to *in-corporate*, to bring into ourselves, the beliefs of others that differ from ours—for it is the blending of these two that causes creative combustion. As surgeon/ writer Leonard Schlain writes in *Art and Physics,* "Opposites are not always contradictions—rather they may be complementary aspects of a higher truth." Or as the quantum physicist Niels Bohr puts it: "Opposite a true statement is a false statement, but opposite a profound truth is another profound truth."

Dissolving our mental barriers to opposing ideas is a heroic act. All our conditioning is against it. We are programmed to believe certain things and to defend these beliefs, but is there truly an absolute truth to defend? We have magazines that cater to the left and magazines that cater to the right, and both are busy proving the other side wrong. Facts are manipulated to serve the purposes of different constituencies, from the relevance of global warming to the needs of hungry children. Just as we can find opposing arguments in our sacred texts, so can we find opposing ideas in the scientific, economic, and political arenas—all based on the same facts.

There is no right or wrong on the level of the absolute. There is only the continual evolution of consciousness, and if we want to participate in this evolution, become an agent in shaping it, then we have to become the vessel in which the opposites fuse and transmute into a higher form. Just as it takes centuries of heat and pressure to transform carbon molecules into precious diamonds, so are we refined in the friction and the fray of human discourse. Underneath all the paragraphs of opposing ideas, there is always a word that rings true to all. Find that word first, then build outward from there.

There is no theoretical solution to the mystery of suffering and evil, but there is the immense field of responsive action toward overcoming what kills human dignity. Elizabeth A. Johnson, CSJ

When I went to the Jerusalem Bible to read from the *Book of Lamentations,* I discovered that the first four poems attributed to the prophet Jeremiah are acrostics. Each verse begins with a letter of the Hebrew alphabet taken in order. I fashioned this Lamentation after our English alphabet.

Lamentation

Anger I find all around me
Blue skies are crowded with bombs
Children are hungry and homeless
Days feel as dark as the night.
Endless are headlines of terror
Frightening the young and the old.
Gaia, our planet, is suffering
How thoughtlessly we destroy our home.
In your presence I kneel in sorrow
Justice has not taken root
Killing occurs east and west
Limping home from the wars come our youth.
Men in power seize all the riches
Nowhere can I look for hope
O how my heart breaks open, crying out for peace in the land.
Prisoners are we to the old ways
Quick to blame and to judge
Ready with arms to do battle
Singing dirges as we march day and night
Triumph of spirit we know not
Unleashed as we are from our souls, we wander, lost in the dark
Violence will turn to vigilance, war will turn to peace
When we see You are not in the heavens, but here in the eyes of our foe.

PRIME (6:00 A.M.)

Evil is my constant companion
its face is broadcast all day long
It is the endless story of separation
All day I repair what they divide.

When I agreed to record a Marry Your Muse creativity program for Sounds True Audio, part of the deal was I'd have an audience. They don't let you read your material. You can have some notes in front of you, but basically you're all alone talking in a room. When I asked if I had a choice about being alone or having an audience, they said yes, of course I could have an audience...so I was confident I could get the juices flowing.

However, when the day came and I walked into the studio, there was a microphone, a music stand for my notes, a small table with tea and lemons, and no audience. "Where *is* everyone?" I asked. "Oh, we thought you were good enough to do it without anyone here. Why don't you try it and see? If it doesn't work, we'll bring in some folks."

I was flabbergasted. "I don't think I'm going to be able to do this," I said. "Who's going to bounce me back? Where will I get my juice?"

"Use the engineer in the booth. Speak to him. He'll be listening. Just try it."

There was a big plate of tinted glass between us and I could barely make out his face, but I put on my earphones, took a look at my notes and started talking to him like his life depended on me. I told him stories. I recited poems. I told jokes. At one time, in the middle of my own story, I was so touched by something I started crying. All alone in that room, I talked myself to tears.

We recorded six hours a day for two days straight. At the end of the recording, the engineer came out of the booth and thanked me for the best session he'd ever done. Turns out I wasn't the only one I brought to tears. We took a long walk together and he repeated to me all the stories that touched him and all the ideas he'll never forget.

Prophets of today speak in ways that move everyone in their midst. They are passionate, thought-provoking, spiritually grounded. They speak with authority. They own their ideas. They themselves are transformed by the fusion of heart and mind, and what ushers forth is an excitement, an energy of confidence that is contagious and convincing because what they are communicating is vital, alive, and pertinent to these times.

Ideas that are born from the union of thought and feeling, that originate out of a desire for synthesis, a diligence to rise above duality, contain within themselves the DNA of transcendence. Carl Jung called emotion the chief source of consciousness. "There is no change from darkness to light or from inertia to movement without emotion," he wrote. The practice of uniting the opposites involves opening the heart as much as the mind. It means feeling our way forward even as we're thinking our way forward, for it is our feelings that rise up like red lights, alerting us to the crossroads of old habits and new choices.

There is a momentary discomfort as we try to find the rightness in another's thinking or perceive the "enemy" as our self. It goes against everything we've ever learned, and it evokes the same kind of emotional withdrawal symptoms that come with every attempt to give up an addiction. We are addicted to dualism because every institution of our lives has promoted this kind of thinking, but none of us can call ourselves free until we rid ourselves of this dangerous habit. The ability to hold two contradictory thoughts simultaneously is not just a matter of true genius; it is a matter of true freedom. If we cannot hear an opposing idea without a negative emotional reaction, we are not free. We are bound to an ideology that we have most likely inherited and never thoroughly examined.

Prophetic leadership is sourced from and rooted in the merging of opposites. Just as a battery is charged by the union of positive and negative forces, just as a child is conceived by the union of a male sperm and female ovum, so does evolutionary thinking emerge from the union of "us" and "them" into a "we."

To race toward certainty, vainglorious.
To claim to know the one and only truth, laughable
for sure; blasphemous perhaps.
There is nowhere to get to and nothing to know
but that all is connected
and what is good for me (and that would be you)
is good, as well, for all the rest.

TERCE (9:00 A.M.)

Though I know not how to combat evil
except to be what it isn't as best I can
Mighty is my readiness for action
My love for good illuminates the night.

Science tells us there are 50-75 trillion cells in our body and our well being depends on every one of them working together for the whole. Likewise, there are 6 billion people on the planet, and the well being of the planet and the collective human family depends on each human working consciously for the benefit of the whole. If it's not good for you, it's not good for me. If it's not good for Nigeria, it's not good for Texas. If it's not good for the rainforest, it's not good for us.

If the body's organs competed with each other like nations and individuals compete, for what they believe to be limited resources, the body would collapse. It is only able to thrive when every cell responds to messages from other cells with an immediate impulse to be of use, to share its life force and send its nutrients where they are needed.

We do damage to the entire human family when we make decisions that serve certain individuals but not the whole. Evolutionary thinking is whole brain thinking. It's body/mind/spirit thinking. It is the art of immersing ourselves so thoroughly in the idea of oneness that the creations, the visions, the solutions we offer the world are clearly in the service of the whole human family. This itself is countercultural, as we have all been born into a world where duality reigns. But this is changing.

We know from science now, if not from our own faith and spiritual awareness, that the notion of separateness is fundamentally wrong, as was the notion of a flat earth or of the earth being the center of the universe. New findings cause a great tumult in the societies called upon to accommodate them, for it is never easy to realign a worldview. And our society now is undergoing a similar upheaval as we bear the breakdown of every system we have created. The old ways are disintegrating before our eyes, as well they might, rooted as they are in the soil of separateness. Profit before people is a concept that should soon be history, for it fails to stand up to the tests of *this* day. Is it good for the whole? Does it harm the system?

It is wrong to let fifteen million children die of hunger every year.

It is wrong to let the world continue to spend on its military in two days what could save the lives of 100 million children.

It is wrong that one out of every eight children under the age of twelve in the U.S. goes to bed hungry every night.

It is wrong that some 46 million African children — nearly half the school-age population — have never set foot in a classroom.

We could extend this list all day long. We know what's wrong. We can feel it in our bones. And though we will probably not topple the dragon of capitalism in our lifetime, we can devote ourselves to reaching out to those wounded by its claws. Once we take it upon ourselves to heal what we can, to work with others on creative solutions, we will evolve ourselves forward into a higher level of thinking, and open ourselves to receive what's coming in from the Intelligence of the Cosmos.

SEXT (NOON)

When I see your pain I ask what I can do.
I light the flame and kneel before its glow
I breathe in guidance from the Mind of Oneness
Some days I sit still, some days I move.

I'm sick of your sacrifices – learn to do good, search for justice,
help the oppressed. Isaiah 1:11

Prophets do not wait in silence. Nor do they wait for others' minds to be opened, or for safe places to speak into. Prophets are the openers of minds who dare say "we" and who know they mean everyone. Some of the greatest thinkers today are in agreement about the power of our consciousness to alter our circumstances. From biologists to business leaders, mystics to medical professionals, philosophers to philanthropists, individuals are speaking out about the role of our thoughts in the unfolding of our realities. Simultaneously, the world of quantum physics is seeding our fertile mindscapes with findings that propel us beyond all known imaginings.

Quantum nonlocality, or nonseparability, is asking us to completely alter our ideas about objects. We can no longer consider objects as independently existing entities. They are interconnected in ways not even conceivable in classical physics. Quantum nonlocality teaches us that particles that were once together in an interaction continue to respond to each other no matter how many miles apart, and at a rate faster than the speed of light. Physicist Menas Kafatos writes: "Nature has shown us that our concept of reality, consisting of units that can be considered as separate from each other, is fundamentally wrong." Since we are composed of cells, molecules, atoms and sub-atomic particles, this makes *each of us* part of one indivisible whole, interconnected and interdependent.

This is hard to put our minds around since we have constructed a society based on myths of duality and separation. Myths are the great overarching stories that we are born into—stories that help us know our place, understand our nature. They are universal in scope, leading us to believe that *this is how it is* for humanity. Myths are stories that bridge our local consciousness to Intelligence at Large. The images they give us reflect our relationship to the eternal, to the earth, and to each other.

In the Neolithic era, people were guided by the creation myth of a Great Mother Goddess who ruled over the natural world and presided over all their earthly activities. Men and women considered themselves children of the Goddess, as they were the children of the women who headed the families and clans. The myth of the Great Mother Goddess connected them to the eternal and guided them in the creation of their culture, art, and social order. Archeological excavations from these cultures have not unearthed weapons and instruments of war, but an abundance of art and artifacts indicating a pervasive reverence for the Great Goddess.

The myths of the Garden of Eden and Cain and Abel reflect the cataclysmic cultural change that erupted when the Bronze Age warriors from the north invaded the peaceful societies of Mesopotamia. With the arrival of these soldiers came male dominance, weaponry, and a war-like mentality. As societies that conceptualized the Goddess as the supreme power in the universe were conquered, the story of the Great Mother was rewritten, and the image of her replaced with one of a wrathful, bearded sky-God.

The myths of dismissal from the Garden, separation from the Divine, and murdering brothers have been the inheritance of Western civilization, and they have had an impact on the creation of our society, just as the Goddess myth had an impact on our Neolithic ancestors and the creation of their society. But myths can and do change over time, and at this time in history, we are undergoing an upheaval as profound as the uprooting of the Goddess and the seeding of patriarchy.

"Humanity is being taken to the place where it will have to choose between suicide and adoration," wrote the Jesuit paleontologist Teilhard de Chardin. The fate of the world, of every child in the world, is in the hands of those of us who populate it, and we are each at that choice point, each responsible every day for actions that move the tipping point one way or another. The matter of evolutionary thinking is an urgent one, as it is time to think anew, to weave the findings of science—of our true interconnectedness, our profound and universal indivisibility—into new myths and stories that feed our souls and inspire adoration.

One of the most revered scientists of all time, Albert Einstein, believed likewise. In a letter written in 1950, he wrote:

> A human being is part of the whole called by us "universe," a part limited in time and space. We experience ourselves, our thoughts and feelings, as something separate from the rest. A kind of optical delusion of consciousness. This delusion is a kind of prison for us, restricting us to our personal desires and to affection for a few persons nearest to us. Our task must be to free ourselves from the prison by widening our circle of compassion to embrace all living creatures and the whole of nature in its beauty. The true value of a human being is determined by the measure and the sense in which they have obtained liberation from the self. We shall require a substantially new manner of thinking if humanity is to survive.

NONE (3:00 PM)

Though sorrow overcomes me I keep moving
day by day I sit with those who hurt
when they speak my soul invites their heart's confession
when they cry, I lay my hands upon their pain.

A few years ago I was visiting my friend Ruby Lee in southern Kentucky. When Sunday morning rolled around, we climbed into her 1972 yellow Oldsmobile and headed off to the Baptist Church. While we were waiting for the service to start, Ruby Lee leaned over and told me, in a hushed voice, to check out the woman at the organ. "She's the minister's wife," she whispered, "but he's having an affair with that blond woman in the second row of the choir. The wife's so mad she's spitting nails and she won't even look at him during the service anymore."

Next thing I knew, the organist was hammering out the processional hymn, her face starched into a sour scowl. The blond in the choir was radiant, singing her heart out and smiling adoringly at the minister as he took his place on the altar. The organist nibbled constantly at her bottom lip and avoided eye contact with anyone in the church.

The balding, overweight minister swaggered to the pulpit like he owned the world. "Brothers and sisters," he bellowed as he raised his arms in a welcoming gesture to the crowd, "today we're here to speak of our enemies, and to follow the Lord's call to love those enemies."

I wasn't sure yet who or what he meant by the enemy, but he said the word with such vehemence it gave me a fright. I looked over at Ruby Lee to see what she made of this, and she was nodding her head in zealous approval. Ruby Lee was seventy-four years old. She had spent nearly every Sunday of her life in this church, and for her, it was business as usual.

As the minister launched into his sermon, his deep voice rose to a fevered pitch and his robe billowed like a mainsail when he flailed his arms. The organist, by this time, was clipping her fingernails, and the blond was sitting on the edge of her choir chair, rapt in devotion to the minister of her dreams. I tried to follow what he was saying, but every time he roared out the word enemy, I just cringed in the pew. After awhile, it was all I heard—enemy this, enemy that.

It was hard for me to stay focused on the subject of enemies since I'd spent my whole life trying not to have any. What I really wanted to do was go up to that pulpit and tell people to get past the whole idea of enemies, because it doesn't serve us anymore. But I stayed where I was, wondering if anyone considered me an enemy, just because of what I think.

When we got into the car after the service, I told Ruby Lee what I was feeling. "Don't you think it's time to move beyond this enemy thing? Don't you think we have to get past what keeps us separate from each other and figure out what we have in common?" She threw her Olds into reverse and backed up right into the chain link fence. "Girl, you sure got some crazy ideas up there. Let's go git lunch."

We headed off to the local hospital for their Sunday brunch, but I couldn't get the minister off my mind. There he was with a captive audience and a chance to make a difference in people's lives. He had all the benefits of theater, with the music, the rituals, the stage of the holy altar. He took a reference from the Bible and created a performance piece on the theme of enemy, and each of us perceived it through our own filters. Had there been critics in the congregation, some would have panned him, others applauded.

On some level, we are all creators whether we intend to be or not. As we perform our lives, there are always people watching us, listening for clues, looking for differences, assessing our actions, our words. We constantly create environments which others enter into and feel either nourished or negated. We create waves of energy that wash over people in our presence—waves that can lull and comfort or lash and damage. We create what our days and nights look like, what work we do, what beauty surrounds us. And on a daily basis, we create the attitude we bring to life and choose whether the door to our heart is open or closed.

We are talking about God. What wonder is it that you do not understand. If you understood, it would not be God. Augustine

I asked the sunrise
I asked the palm and the redwood
I asked Lake Ontario and the Pacific Ocean
I asked the Adirondacks, Kilimanjaro, and the Himalayas
I asked Calcutta, Juneau, and Jerusalem
I asked the Colorado River and the River Jordan
I asked the Mediterranean, the Baltic, and the Sea of Galilee
I asked the tornado, the tsunami, the hurricanes A-Z,
I asked Abraham, Mohammed, Gaia, Buddha, Ramakrishna, and Jesus
I asked Mary Magdalene, Mary Oliver, Mother Teresa, Sojourner Truth,
Gloria Steinem, Anita Hill, Audre Lorde
I asked Joan of Arc, Marie Antoinette, Catherine of Siena
I asked Nigeria, Bolivia, Egypt
I asked the setting sun, the rising tide, the waning moon
I looked each of them square in the eye
and asked, not once, but twice,
to be perfectly clear.
And each, in their own inimitable way,
looked back squarely and said "Yes..."
"Yes and no."

VESPERS (SUNSET)

Terrorism seeps into my mindscape
I rage, I cry, I kneel
How can I stop this hateful action?
Be what it is not all day long.

There's no debating that we live in a shocking world. Nothing has brought
this home more than reality TV. It doesn't take more than five minutes of chan-
nel-surfing to come upon at least one or two scenes that make you wonder
what is going on out there. Shocking, indeed. And then there's awe. Shock and
awe. Surf through a few more channels and you'll come across families losing
hundreds of pounds together, teams building new homes for people, volunteers

rescuing animals from terrible conditions. You'll find yourself welling up, feeling proud of the human family, wanting to send thank-you cards out by the hundreds.

In her book *Moments of Being*, Virginia Woolf writes on the value of shock:

> *I go on to suppose that the shock-receiving capacity is what makes me a writer. I hazard the explanation that a shock is at once in my case followed by the desire to explain it. I feel that I have had a blow; but it is not, as I thought as a child, simply a blow from a enemy hidden behind the cotton wool of daily life; it is or will become a revelation of some order; it is a token of some real thing behind appearance; and I make it real by putting it into words.*

> *It is only by putting it into words that I make it whole; this wholeness means that it has lost its power to hurt me; it gives me, perhaps because by doing so I take away the pain, a great delight to put the severed parts together. Perhaps this is the strongest pleasure known to me. It is the rapture I get when in writing I seem to be discovering what belongs to what; making a scene come right; making a character come together.*

> *From this I reach what I might call a philosophy; at any rate, it is a constant idea of mine. that behind the cotton wool is hidden a pattern; that we—I mean all human beings—are connected with this: that the whole world is a work of art; that we are parts of the work of art. Hamlet or a Beethoven quartet is the truth about this vast mass that we call the world. But there is no Shakespeare, there is no Beethoven; certainly and emphatically there is no God; we are the words; we are the music; we are the thing itself. And I see this when I have a shock.*

It is a great help to have people put things into words. You may not agree with everything Woolf says, but she gives you something to rub against. She gives you a measuring stick, somewhere to start, to see if how it is for you is in anyway similar. This is how we come to know ourselves. And awe plays a similar role: it wakes us up to something. Only with awe, our attention shifts toward the collective. It is beyond the personal. Awe causes the oxytocin in our systems to increase, which makes us feel loving toward others.

In a study on awe, UC Berkeley psychologist Dacher Keltner and his team had a group of people complete 20 sentences beginning with "I am..." Half the group completed it while facing a full-size replica of a Tyrannosaurus rex skeleton in the Life Sciences building on campus. The other half completed it while facing a hallway. The upshot was, the people looking at the T. rex were three times likelier to describe themselves as part of something larger than those who completed the quest- ions facing a hallway. The feeling of "Wow! There's something bigger than me" can be the thing that spurs one into action, according to Keltner, who suggests John Muir's transcendent experiences in the outdoors were what inspired him to create the Sierra Club.

Living in a world of shock and awe is an opening for myth-making, for meaning-making as we try to make sense of the world and share what we're making of it with the people we love. Just as Moses responded to the evils of his day, as Jeremiah wrote his Lamentations, as David created the Psalms, as Noah built the ark, as Buddha and Jesus told stories, meditated, and modeled generosity, it is our turn now to shine our light, to find our medium, to create a mosaic from the fractured fragments of a world pushing forward in an evolutionary advance.

Why did you choose to be here now?
Can you remember that thing you came here to do?

Not to transmit an experience is to betray it. Elie Wiesel, Holocaust survivor

Lamentation #2

A world once verdant is suffering, her oceans and rivers now poisoned
Blind men rule with no mercy, and the sighted refuse to speak.
Children cry out with hunger, their tongues parched for water that's pure
Do you hear the cry of my wailing? Like a widow I mourn day and night.

Enemies spring from our ignorance, armies rise up from our fear
Forgetting we started as family, we draw boundaries and call brothers foes.
Great are you and All Glorious, creator of heaven and earth
HaShem, Holy Mother, Our Father,
I bow before you in tears.

Judge us not, but move us forward, past this era of weapons and war
Knead us like dough in your hands, shape us into servants of truth.
Low is my head bowed in shame for all the ways we betray you
Money and might have consumed us, our forests we're trading for meat.

Nowhere are children safe from the clutch of capital's claw
Our skin is parched and dry, because of the heat of our greed.
Politicians betray the people, religions have forgotten their role
Quiet are the voices of reason while the hateful shout all night long.

Restore our sight, that we see our enemies more clearly
Send us light and remove our blinders,
Though we fear the unknown, guide us toward it
Until we find our common center hope is lost

Violence and terror are rampant, in your name we destroy and kill
We bring guns not bread to the altar, our wine is the blood of our kin.
You have made a cosmos of grandeur, in our hands is this one world to shape
Zealots of love awaken! Let your kindness spill over the land.

COMPLINE (9:00 P.M.)

Adoration I exhale with every breath
for the mysteries of life and love and loss
I cannot know the Source nor can I name it
Though it is in me as I in It.

> We mould the best and the most powerful among us, taking them while they're still young, like lion cubs, and with charms and incantations we subdue them into slavery, telling them that one is supposed to get no more than his fair share, and that this is what is fair and just. But I believe that if there were to be a man whose nature was up to it, one who had shaken off, torn apart, and escaped all this, who had trampled underfoot our documents, our trickery and charms, and all those laws that are against nature, then he, the slave, would rise up; and be revealed as our master, and then the justice of nature would shine out…
>
> Callicles in the *Gorgias* by Plato (429-347 BCE)

Consider what you learned when you were young about authority and who should have it; what you were told about being a male or a female; about people of other cultures, colors, and religions, about the poor, about your body, about your sexuality. Get a visual image of all those moments, when all those values were handed to you, and when you, in your state of pure innocence, received them like commandments carved into stone. No one meant us harm. They were handing down values that were handed to them in the same way, with the same good intentions.

Our parents, our teachers, our ministers, priests, and rabbis were shaping us in their image so that we would fit in, conform to the contours of the established culture. They wanted us to be safe. They were not promoting spiritual intelligence, not engaging us in questions of why and how. They were attempting to contain our imaginations so that we wouldn't venture out too far beyond the fold. And step by step, many of us have had to teach ourselves how to think independently, how to let go of harmful beliefs, how to establish our own values based on our life experiences. This is an ongoing process and one that involves a whole systems approach —our minds, our bodies, our feelings, our faith.

With the onslaught of information coming our way on a daily basis, creative thinking has become an aerobic exercise. It requires a constant opening of the heart which tends to close down in the face of inhumanity. Wanting to protect ourselves from images of starving children, terrorized nations, crime-ridden cities, we resist looking. Our emotions recede into a safer place, denial jams our channels of expression, chokes our imagination, and our thoughts become hostage to fear.

The only access we have to our authenticity is the pathway through the heart, and we must keep this channel open, at all costs. We must look deeply into our world, into its heartbreak, into the eyes of our sisters and brothers, and let these images awaken our senses, expand our awareness, and jolt our memories back to the truth of our oneness. It is not altruism, not charity, not selflessness that will open the gates to our own magnitude. It is awareness. And when awareness is fleshed out in the experience of our lives, it culminates in the events of relationship, of collaboration and cooperation.

This is true even in the natural world, as is illustrated by the behavior of slime mold amoeba who live out most of their four day life spans as single-celled animals in search of bacteria. Since they only move half an inch in twenty-four hours, they quickly devour all the food within reach, so their next strategy is to excrete a hormone-like substance that sends out chemical pulses about eight minutes apart. Other amoebae sense these distress signals and start emitting their own as they move toward the source. As many as a hundred thousand amoebae stream toward each other until they merge into a multicellular "slug" where they share their DNA and create the next generation of offspring. The new amoebae hibernate in spores until they receive signals from nearby food molecules that it is time to end their hibernation and enter the world as single-celled amoeba again. Isolation is death. Relationship is survival, resilience, regeneration.

It is our relationships that sustain us personally—heartening us, empowering us, comforting us. It is our relationships that ground us, support us, inspire us— even in the darkest times. And collectively, as we search for solutions to our global undoing—the poverty that eats at us, the health crises that are decimating populations, the grave imbalances between those who have and those who have not—it will be in relationships that our answers will unfold and our fears subside.

We learn from science, from religion, from the arts that we are intricately connected, but how is this reflected in our myths? Where are the stories of this? Where are the pictures we need to see of ourselves? Where are our mirrors? We are blasting images of American culture around the world that few of us subscribe to or align with. We are saying to the hungry, to the hordes of unemployed, to those we have never helped to educate: "Look here, see how rich we are, see how liberated we are, see all the stuff we have, all the power we have," with no regard, no insight as to what impact this might have on the spirits of those people.

A Nigerian prince once said, "If you don't share your wealth with us, we'll share our poverty with you." What in the world are you doing to share your wealth?

Psalm #2

As the deer that yearns for running streams
so do I yearn for a peaceful world
My tears flow like blood as forests burn
my heart breaks open as bombs explode.

It is said "we are gods"
and the "light of the world"
yet we kill and spread darkness
with Your name on our lips.

Did You not say "judge not
and be merciful?"
I cover my face in shame
at the hatred in our midst.

For thousands of years
we have called out Your name

singing Adonai, Allah, Redeemer, God
while Your words say
the kingdom is spread out before us
and our kindness to others is kindness to You.

We cry for your help
though your hands are ours
we call for your mercy
though we are its agents.

Lo! do I mourn for our ignorance and greed
I wail through the night as bombs light the sky
yet love songs of birds rouse me at dawn
the heat of your sun awakens me.

O Mystery of Mystery,
though your ways bewilder me
though I wander through my days
crying "what shall I do?"
Your voice drifts in on the morning breeze:
"Be who you are. The doing will get done.
Love what you see. I am that, I am."

In the 1920s, Teilhard de Chardin, referred to the noosphere as the "thinking envelope of the planet." The noosphere is the third in a succession of phases of development of the Earth, after the geosphere (inanimate matter) and the biosphere (biological life). Just as the emergence of life fundamentally transformed the geosphere, the emergence of human cognition fundamentally transforms the biosphere. It is also currently being researched as part of the Princeton Global Consciousness Project.

While we can't scientifically prove there's such a thing as global consciousness, there is an abundance of research that confirms the power of collective consciousness. Many studies have found that just one percent of a population practicing transcendental meditation (TM) is sufficient to bring about a significant reduction in crime, sickness, and accidents, a phenomenon researchers call the "Maharishi Effect." An interest among sociologists and criminologists generated by those results led to a highly publicized "National Demonstration Project to Reduce Violent Crime and Improve Governmental Effectiveness" in Washington, DC from June 7 to July 30, 1993. According to quantum physicist John Hagelin, author of *Manual for a Perfect Government,* the $6 million scientific demonstration, which involved four thousand participants over a period of two months, was one of the largest and most rigorously designed sociological experiments in history.

The prediction of a 20 percent drop in crime and the research methodology to be used was presented in advance to a twenty-seven member project review board consisting of scientists, government leaders, and the District of Columbia police department. The coherence-creating group consisted of one thousand meditators on June 7 and increased incrementally to four thousand by the end of the project on July 30. By the end of the demonstration project, violent crime dropped sharply by more than 23 percent. Later analysis determined that the drop in crime could not be attributed to temperature, precipitation, changes in police surveillance, weekend effects, or trends in the data.

Hagelin reports on well-documented experiments in the Middle East of groups of TM meditators who were able to produce a 34 percent reduction in war intensity and a 76 percent reduction in war deaths during the Lebanon war. In 2003, the highly respected Journal of Offender Rehabilitation devoted all four quarterly issues entirely to studies demonstrating that the TM program is effective in treating and preventing criminal behavior, as well as reducing international conflicts and terrorism. This is what we are moving toward—the ability to use the powers of our consciousness in a more public way for a more public good. Evolutionary creativity at its best.

CHAPTER FIVE FRIDAY

If we can stay with the tension of opposites long enough—sustain it, be true to it—we can sometimes become vessels within which the divine opposites come together and give birth to a new reality. Marie Louise von Franz (1915-1998)

NON-DUALITY

I was eating dinner with friends at a small Italian restaurant when three men with guns walked through the door. "Get up!" they shouted as they approached our table. We were stunned and sat frozen in our seats, none of us moving. Two of them walked through the swinging doors into the kitchen and the other came closer with his gun pointing. "Keep your eyes down and get into the kitchen, now! And take your bags!" By now it had sunk in that this was really happening and we all stood up and headed into the kitchen, the gunman behind us.

"Don't anybody look," he warned. "Just lie down on the floor and keep your eyes shut." We did as he said, and took our places on the floor, along with the kitchen staff, who were already lying face down. He told the men to put their wallets on the floor, then instructed all of us to remove our jewelry and watches and put them on the floor next to us. "Keep your eyes shut," he kept shouting while his cohorts collected the wallets and jewelry.

They went into the office next, while one kept guard over us. I heard someone go through the swinging door, and then there was a long silence. I thought they had left, so I lifted up my head and looked toward the door, just as one pushed it open. He saw me looking and came at me with his gun pointed at my head, shouting "I told you to keep your eyes shut!"

"I can't see anything without my glasses," I said, burrowing my head under my arms, and at that point, the strangest thing happened. I saw the whole scene from above, as if I were suspended from the ceiling. As I viewed our bodies sprawled out on the greasy kitchen floor, powerless and terrified, I heard a voice in my head whisper, "This is what we've come to. This is what human beings are now doing to other human beings." And out of my eyes, tears began to fall onto the floor.

In this moment, my local brain and global mind became one. The local me was the victim, paralyzed with fear, worried for my life, grieving over an image seen by the global me—an image of my own tribe run amok. From that upper view, I was a witness, not a victim. I was the many, not the one—the "we," not the "I."

Years later, as I think back on this event, I find that it gave me a metaphor for understanding the distinction between global and local, and seeing that they are two sides of one coin. My reality is simultaneously local and global. I am at once the witness and the witnessed, the creator of experience and the one who experiences it. I am like the cell in the organism—offering my vitality to the whole and taking my vitality from it. A singular and unique entity, I bring to the whole what no one else can bring, and doing that, I find my place in the family of things.

It is at the intersection of local brain and global mind that our creative fire is ignited and fanned. It is here, when these poles are brought together, that original thoughts are conceived and born, that the future enters into us before it happens. It is the recognition of our oneness that causes the quantum leap to a higher level of thinking. Einstein wrote: "The world that we have made as a result of the level of thinking we have done thus far creates problems which cannot be solved by the same level of thinking in which they were created." Until we shift into global mind thinking we cannot solve the problems that we have created with local brain thoughts.

We have built a world based on our separation from each other and it is unsustainable. To create a world that is just and sustainable, we must design and build with our oneness in mind, asking ourselves at every point, *What is best for the whole?* And that is why visionaries are needed so desperately now—because they operate from this place, they dwell in the awareness of oneness, and this consciousness radiates from their very beings, affecting everyone in their midst.

When I think of prophetic leaders, I think of those who draw us after them, whose energy field, like that of a magnet, extends beyond the body itself, attracting others to the brightness of their light. It is true for all of us, that our heart energy precedes us as we navigate through life, extending beyond us as an aura potent enough to affect those in our path—but there is something particularly uplifting about the energy of people who are aware of the threads that connect us all and whose work in the world reflects this knowing.

That we have an effect on others is a matter of fact; the *kind* of effect we have on others is a matter of consciousness. We can radiate blessings and light or negativity and darkness. It is in our best interests to be mindful of our energy as we scatter it about, because thoughts can produce effects only of the same nature. Kindness to others favors a nervous system that is kind to itself, says the *Bhagavad Gita*.

This is global mind thinking. It is countercultural, for we have been trained to think otherwise, but it is the very essence of non-dualistic thinking. It sees beyond the artificial boundaries that our cultures have put in place. Before we can manage anything or anyone in the outside world, we must first learn to manage our energy and thoughts, to synchronize our mind and our emotions for optimal performance. Then we will be ready to enter higher levels of consciousness, increase our intuitive capacities, and tap into a creativity greater than we have ever known.

True genius is the ability to hold two contradictory thoughts simultaneously without losing your mind. Charles Beaudelaire

Can you evolve your own thinking process beyond duality, beyond "right and wrong," beyond "good and evil?" Can you accept that we are all right, only partly so? That we need to mix our thoughts up with others to come up with the greatest variety of solutions, the highest synthesis of consciousness?

MATINS (MIDNIGHT)

We grow up in a world that keeps things separate
Science is a thousand miles from faith
The right wing and the left are far divided
Though the angel cannot fly without them both.

Years ago, when I was making a cross-country trip interviewing small town folks about their values, I made my way to the homestead of a friend's mother in Kentucky. Her name was Babe. She was seventy-two and lived with her brother, Arthur, who was eighty-eight. When I drove up the long driveway, Babe was sitting on the porch, rocking in her rattan rocker. She waved me up, fetched me a glass of lemonade, and regaled me with tales for the next few hours. When we went into the house, Babe showed me around, saying "This is Arthur's room," at the entrance to the living room. Arthur was out somewhere, so I hadn't met him, but as soon as I saw all the John Birch literature on his coffee table, I knew all I needed to know. This man was an ultra-conservative, militaristic, fundamentalist and I didn't want to have anything to do with him. In fact, I was glad he was gone.

Halfway through supper with Babe, in walked Arthur, big as life and gruff as a bear. Babe babbled on about how I was an author, writing this big article on values, and how he ought to talk to me. I nearly choked on my okra. The last thing I wanted to do was talk to Arthur, but he told me to meet him on the porch at eight o'clock the next morning, and he'd tell me whatever I needed to know.

Bright and early the next morning, I ventured out to the porch with my notebook and pen. Arthur was already there, with an old gray cap on his head and a hand-carved cane in tow. "Come on," he barked, setting off across the lawn. "Get a move on."

"I thought I was going to interview you," I said.

"Can't you walk and talk? Hurry up! Times a wastin'."

Leaving my notebook in the chair, I took off after Arthur, agitated already.

He started talking about the lumber business he used to own, what kind of trees were on the property, how he knew the land like the back of his hand. The he stopped in his tracks and pointed at a tree with his cane. "Look over there at that walnut tree," he said. "Can you tell me how in the world that tree spits out those walnuts that are so hard I can't crack 'em with my hands? Even them squirrels have to crack 'em on a rock just to get 'em open. What power's loose in the world that can make that happen year after year?"

We walked a bit farther, then he stopped again, pointing his cane at the nearby garden. "Look over there at those rows of corn. Why, I just planted those seeds a while ago, and now look, row after row of perfect stalks, with the silkiest golden tassels you ever did see. And do you know what you're gonna find when you pull off those tassels and husk those ears? You're gonna find row after row of golden kernels, all lined up perfect. You tell me, girl, what power's loose in this world that can make that happen?"

I was amazed. This was a man who I'd taken for my opposite. A man I didn't want to talk with. A man I'd boxed into the category "other," and written off as a person to avoid. And now he was ushering me around his land, opening his heart, unfolding the details of his love affair with nature. We walked for two hours, through the woods, down to the creek, across the meadows, and all the while Arthur spoke of the birds, the flowers, the maples, the oaks, as if they were miracles of life going unnoticed. My listening was a vessel for his secrets, a temple for his sacred thoughts. My questions drew the light from his deepest places. My laughter met his gruffness and turned it into joy. We were yin and yang, Arthur and I, and on that two-hour walk we fell in love.

He insisted I stay a few more days, and every morning we'd walk the land, as Arthur talked about trees and nature, his personal beliefs, his troubled life. We had taken up emotional residence in each other's being and it was no longer possible to think of him as "other." Arthur had become my brother in spirit, my friend, and a mirror to myself. His opinions, different as they were from my own, were easier to understand, knowing their context and how they were formed. I had to think more broadly with Arthur in my life, and for this I'm grateful.

Before I left, Arthur confessed to his lifelong dream of seeing the Great Sequoia trees out west. "I waited too long, it'll never happen now, but that's something I dreamed of since I was a boy."

"Arthur, it's not too late," I said. "You can still get there."

"No, it's too late," he insisted. "My own damn fault. I just waited too long."

After that, when I was on the road, I'd always look for postcards with pictures of trees. "Dear Arthur," I'd write. "It's not too late. There's still time. Get to the redwoods! Love, Jan." I must have sent him dozens of cards.

Months went by, and I finally made it back to my home in Syracuse. When I collected my mail, what a surprise to find a postcard from Arthur, from the Sequoia National Forest. "Dear Jan, If it hadn't been for you, I'd never have made it. These trees make me cry like a baby. What power's loose in this world? Love, Arthur."

My relationship with Arthur lasted a few years before he died, and it taught me one of my biggest lessons: that there is a great advantage to exploring the minds of people whose opinions are different from mine. While there is a kind of friction as opposing thoughts rub against each other, there is also the potential for creative fire that comes with that friction. And that's what we're after.

Sonnet for the Return of Sight

If ever in the throes of troubled thought
I notice not the loveliness of night
nor find within its darkness what I ought:
the flame that's only glimpsed at second sight—

If words of mine contain no joy nor faith,
If mystery and wonder take their leave,
Then come and lay me down on Heaven's lathe.
Remove my blinders; these I will not grieve.

Restore my sight, that deeper things I see,
the light within the dark, beneath the veil,
let fears and shadows not bewilder me,
when lo! I come upon the Holy Grail.

For you are all I ever seek to find
Shine through this dark, O God, my Love Sublime.

An Arabian Story

A man died. He had seventeen camels and three sons and he left a will in which, when it was opened and read, it was said that one half of the camels should go to the first son, one third to the second and one ninth to the third. The sons were confused — what to do? Seventeen camels: one half is to go to the first son — is one to cut one camel in two? And that too won't solve much because then one third has to go to the second. That too won't solve much: one ninth has to go to the third. Almost all the camels would be killed.

So they went to the man of the town who was most knowledgeable: the Mulla, the scholar, the mathmetician. He thought hard, he tried hard, but he couldn't find any solution because mathematics is mathematics. He said, "I have never divided camels in my life, this whole thing seems to be foolish. But you will have to cut them. If the will is to be followed exactly then the camels have to be cut, they have to be divided. The sons were not ready to cut the camels. So what to do? Then somebody suggested, "It is better that you go to someone who knows something about camels, not about mathematics." So they went to the sheikh of the town who was an old man, uneducated but wise through experience. They told him their problem.

The old man laughed. He said, "Don't be worried. It is simple." He loaned one of his own camels to them — now there were eighteen camels — and then he divided. Nine camels were given to the first and he was satisfied, perfectly satisfied. Six camels were given to the second, one third; he was also perfectly satisfied. And two camels were given to the third, one ninth; he was also satisfied. One camel was left. That was loaned. He took his camel back and said, "You can go."

Fifty years from now, your descendents will look back at your life and wonder what you were thinking, that you stood by and allowed so many injustices to occur all around you. Will it look to them like you just didn't care? Like you didn't have enough intelligence to figure things out and try to improve your society? Will you appear to them like all those Germans who lived near the concentration camps, saw the ashes fill the air, watched the trains come and go, and yet never did a thing to right the wrong? Will you be an ancestor they will be proud to have in their family tree? Will you stand out as a person who made a difference?

LAUDS (SUNRISE)

I and the Beloved are One
With news as good as that
No one has to tell me twice to
Laugh out loud till I cry for joy.

We let go of the old to discover the new, as we let go of illusions to discover the real. The way to awareness is the way of subtraction, of letting go, one by one, of our fears, our doubts, our prejudices, our judgments, our inherited notions of how it should be, who deserves what, who is to blame. What's happening in the world is a result of our collective input. The morning headlines are the news that we are making as a whole human family, by what we do and what we fail to do. Each one of us is a co-creator of the culture we are immersed in, and if we want to see change, we can make change by changing ourselves, our thinking, and our destructive habits.

Blame is not useful. Polarization is not useful. Bitterness and negativity are not useful. What's useful in these perilous times is deep thought and dialogue. What's useful is a willingness to speak from our hearts, to say out loud what we hunger for, what we're willing to live for, and what it is we can no longer abide. We are attendants at the wake of the old way, and each of us—through our actions, our thoughts, our work and relationships—is midwifing a new world into existence. This is our destiny, our meaning, our purpose, and when we come to our days with this awareness, when we sense the oak in the acorn of our beings, then we will have the energy to move mountains and shift the tides.

Transformation originates in people who see a better way or a fairer world, people who reveal themselves, disclose their dreams, and unfold their hopes in the presence of others. And this very unfolding, this revelation of raw, unharnessed desire, this deep longing to be a force for good in the world is what inspires others to feel their own longings, to remember their own purpose, and to act, perhaps for the first time, in accordance with their inner spirit.

As individuals, the greatest courage that is called for is the courage to be real. When we are real, it melts the frozen places in ourselves and others. It opens the passageways between our hearts and our brains, thaws the blockages that constrain our imagination, and carries us down to our wellsprings of wis-

126

dom. The solutions to our crises are already here. They exist in our relationships, in our stories, in our unfolding forgiveness, and it is through the expression of these things that we will one day live into the answers we seek.

The creativity that is required at this time is a creativity of generosity and magnanimity, a creativity surging with an illuminating power that will help us shatter our cultural constraints. To be constructive, it is not the answers we need, but the spiritual wherewithal to convene the circles, articulate the questions, frame the conversation, and direct attention to the issues that matter. It is the community that will rise up in response to our calling—joyful to be invited, heartened to be involved—and it is the community that will lead us beyond our fears and into a reality brighter than our wildest imaginings.

Song: I and the Mother Are One

I and the Mother are one,
Like the sky and the moon and sun
Like the ocean and stream,
Like the dreamer and dream,
I and the Mother are one.

I and the Mother Are one
Like the sky and the moon and sun
Like the blizzard and snow,
Like the river and flow
I and the Mother are one.

I and the Mother Are one
Like the sky and the moon and sun.
Like the earth and the sea,
Like the branch and the tree
I and the Mother are one.

I and the Mother are one,
Like the sky and the moon and sun,

Like the blanket and warm
Like the thunder and storm
I and the Mother are one.

I and the Mother are one,
Like the sky and the moon and sun,
Like the orchard and vine,
Like the grape and the wine,
I and the Mother are one.

I and the Mother are one,
Like the sky and the moon and sun,
Like the part and the whole
Like the body and soul,
I and the Mother are one.

The test of a first-rate intelligence is the ability to hold two opposed ideas in the mind at the same time, and still retain the ability to function. One should, for example, be able to see that things are hopeless and yet be determined to make them otherwise. F. Scott Fitzgerald

PRIME (6:00 A.M.)

There's a simple test to see if one's enlightened
or at least if one is on the path to light
The question is: can you live one day without thinking
that someone you encountered wasn't you?

It takes more than a vision to make a visionary. It takes a rigorous discipline of mindfulness and a meticulous undoing of old habits. It requires the capacity to not simply withstand the tension of opposites, but to become the mechanism for their transformation, to contain and direct the power that is generated as they fuse and ignite. Just as a battery cable needs to be connected to the positive and negative poles to give it the power to recharge a dead battery, so it is with us. If we learn to bring the opposites together in our own lives—to welcome ideas that differ, to embrace people from different cultures and creeds—then we learn, as well, the alchemy of evolutionary creativity.

The boy in me wants fame and notoriety
the girl in me looks for people in need

the light in me wants to light up the world
the shadow in me wants to close all my doors

the yin in me longs for silence
the yang wants to throw parties and drink too much wine

the seeker in me runs here and there calling out for God
the mystic in me waltzes with the Beloved all day.

Terce (9:00 a.m.)

You needn't know the answers to begin
Do not wait for perfect clarity to start
Just set out with goodness as your goal
Imperfect acts surpass no acts at all.

Answering the questions that are besieging us now calls for a plunging of our whole beings into the dilemmas presented in every morning newspaper. Relying solely on sacred texts is an invitation for chaos and polarization. There will always be those who want to "turn the other cheek" and those who want "an eye for an eye," and each will be "right" according to their choice. Fear is in the air now because each side is building a formidable case for its rightness, and the energy that might be spent on solving the problems is going into proving the other side wrong. The butterfly will never get off the ground if the right wing is at war with the left wing.

The answers that we are seeking lie *between* the right and left and the only way to access them is to move toward the other, to re-pair the opposites. But one look at our culture—from our religions to our media to our politics—reveals a history of opposition, a "divide and conquer" disposition.

The Internet and the media are the nervous system of the global body and our synapses are more connected now than ever before. Years ago we had to rely on *National Geographic* for pictures of our brothers and sisters from far away, but now we see them every day on CNN. I have passed by bamboo huts in the middle of a rice field outside Bangkok and seen the flickering blue light of a television screen. We see them. They see us. Our glimpses into each others' lives are giving shape to the greatest questions of our times and we will not find our answers in books or facts or science or religion or anything than has been constructed by minds from another age. The problems we face can only be solved when we stop looking behind us for answers and begin looking within and around us. Our insights will come from communion and convergence, and this must happen both within ourselves and in our relationships with others.

It is time now to re-pattern our thought processes and disavow all notions of our powerlessness as individuals. It is the thoughts and actions of individuals that have created the world we experience today and it will be the thoughts and actions of individuals that create the world we will live in tomorrow. We are those individuals and this is our time to break through every wall that has kept us from wholeness, every border than has kept us from "the other," and every belief that has silenced and disempowered us.

What makes non-dualistic thinking evolutionary is that it synthesizes the outer and the inner and arrives at a new awareness that encompasses them both. It is a dynamic process that incorporates—from the Latin *incorporare,* meaning to embody, to bring together into a single whole—thoughts we receive from the outer world and insights we hold in our inner world, gleaned from our experience, our intuitions, our sensibilities. Evolutionary thinking does not favor the letter of the law over the spirit of the law, or vice versa, but shapes a new and creative thought-form from the basic elements of the two. This is the alchemy of the creative process. It does not set hydrogen against oxygen, but incorporates the two and yields water.

Think of someone you consider to be the "enemy." How is this person's thinking opposite from yours? What idea might you have in common?

SEXT (NOON)

The young terrorist is inside me
The Wall Street profiteer is here, too
The despotic ruler breathes through my lungs
Can I still spread love all day long?

In 1983, I left Syracuse, New York for a peace pilgrimage around the world. I had saved $5000, had a slideshow on the peace movement in my backpack, and was going to go to as many countries as I could, show my slides to as many people as I could, and create as many occasions for us to come together and talk about what peace-making means to us as I could until I ran out of money. My first stop was Japan.

I ended up visiting a community in the Japanese Alps founded by a Roman Catholic priest turned Buddhist monk. Ten people lived in this community, and they gathered in the chapel every morning before dawn for Lauds and meditation. After that, we sang Gregorian chant, then had Mass. We sat in a circle around the altar, which was merely a cloth on the floor in the center of the room with a chalice, candle, plate, and water bowl on it. After Mass and breakfast, everyone worked silently in the fields during the day. At five o'clock, we stopped for Vespers, more meditation, dinner, and an evening talk by Father Oshida. At night, I immersed myself in Buddhist literature, trying to get an understanding of this spiritual tradition and the master of the East who preceded Jesus by five centuries.

After a few days, I was in a quandary. While my western Christian roots inspired this pilgrimage with its mandate for action, the Buddhist way seemed to be more about silence and meditation. They both made sense and I was torn between the two. I wondered if I should give up the whole idea of making this pilgrimage and just go home, sit quietly in meditation, and be at peace knowing that all things were unfolding perfectly.

Every night ten of us shared a meal together, then sat in a circle and discussed issues that had some bearing on our spiritual lives. Being a spiritual adventurer, I was delighted to delve into Buddhist philosophy, eager to see what it asked for and offered, but I experienced some conflict when I tried to mesh the principles of an inner-centered Buddhism with my outer-directed Christianity.

Though I had long abandoned affiliation with any religious institution, I found that immersing myself in an unfamiliar religion exposed the underpinnings of my own religious values. Until I was in a Buddhist context, I could not see the claim that Christianity had on my life—a claim that was not so much intellectual as cellular, propelling my movement if not my conscious thoughts. While the Buddhists around me were calmly seeking to be and accept, I was relentlessly seeking to do and change. As they sat in quiet embrace of the world's reality, I floundered about noisily, trying to alter it.

My call was a version of the Biblical mandate to "go and teach all nations," while theirs was a call to stillness and silence. But what was the right way? Which path should I travel? Was this trip around the world, this peace pilgrimage I had started only weeks before, a futile gesture, a waste of time that would be better spent elsewhere? This was a conflict I could not resolve.

One day, while doing chores with Father Oshida, I asked if he could help me with my latest dilemma. "Of course," he said, tending to the wheat sheaves he was spreading out to dry. "What trouble are you having?"

132

All my life, I told him, when given a choice, I had tried to choose what I thought Jesus would choose. I had tried to be selfless, as I was taught, and to do what I could to make life better for those around me, which had led to a life of social activism. Now, I confessed, I didn't know what to do. On the one hand, I believed that one person could make a difference in the world. But being in a Buddhist environment led me to question whether it was better to be mindful and accepting of things as they are, or better to get out there and try to make some changes.

"What I'm trying to say," I blurted, "is that I don't know what to do or how to be anymore. I don't even know if I should continue this trip." Father Oshida continued to lay out the grain, nodding his head and arranging each sheaf so it faced the sun. "We are not called to be like Christ, but to BE Christ. And we do this by being most truly ourselves—not by trying to be one way or another, but by being fully aware of who we are and responding to all things from that awareness."

"How do I know if I'm doing it well?"

"You know because you are at peace with yourself, having responded to the voice of your own heart."

"But doesn't God want us to think of others first and take care of them before ourselves? Aren't we supposed to be doing what we can to make the world a better place?"

"The point is not to convert the world, but to convert our souls to God, to see everything as the Incarnation. It is not to interpret things literally with our minds, but to go deeper and experience wisdom. Sometimes when we do that, it takes us away from the world, into our own quiet places where we are not always available to people. It is from that silence that we learn what is next for us, where our path is leading, and how we can be of service."

"But how do I know if I should continue my trip or go home?"

"You ask what brings you joy and do that. You'll know you're doing the right thing by the joy it will bring you. That's how the heart is guided."

I spent the next day in silence, reconsidering values that had shaped the contours of my life. I wrestled with the question of being and doing, searching not for what was right but for what seemed the better fit. I reflected about time, pondering when to give and when to take it, what I owed to myself, what I owed to others. I questioned the sacrosanct notion that the needs of others were more important than my own, and with the care of a gardener committed to life, I started pruning beliefs that no longer felt right.

Adding East to my West, I burrowed down into a faith that had taught me to reach out, discovering that depth was as crucial as height, and silence as vital as speech. As I began to understand the distinction between being Christ and being *like* Christ, I felt a certain relief, no longer needing to labor over what someone else would do in a particular situation, but trusting my own instincts as I honored myself along with the others. My task was to transform the inner voice into outward action, to go to the desert when necessary, to attend to others when that was the call. It was not a matter of putting others before myself out of some selfless striving, but of remaining true to the work I am called to.

That night, on my little cot in my simple cell, I decided to keep going on my journey. I didn't have to choose between Christianity and Buddhism. I could synthesize them, incorporate both into my practice, so I would be a Whole that contained the two—silence *and* speaking, meditation *and* action. My pilgrimage then became an act of living prayer. It wasn't about changing the world or changing myself. It was about experiencing myself as an incarnation of a great force, and being as true to my heart as I could be.

NONE (3:00 PM)

The path is short to heaven
The kingdom is spread all around
There is no one to seek, no place to go
Every morning we awaken to it All.

A few years ago, I awoke in the middle of the night with the word "livingkindness" in my head. I reached for my journal and wrote it down. For days I tried to figure out what it was supposed to mean, but the best I could come up with was that it was a new iteration of the concept "lovingkindness" which is found throughout the Hebrew Bible, the Christian Old Testament, and also in Buddhist practice and the Bahá'í Faith. Lovingkindness, I reasoned, was the concept of agape love, a love of compassionate fellowship. Livingkindness, I thought, could be the actual *practice* of that love—the music to the lovingkindness score.

It occurred to me I could call a circle and get people involved, but I was determined to find a collaborator who was excited about co-creating something new. It felt like a new movement was taking shape inside me—a grassroots philanthropy movement, a way for creatives to use their imagination in small ways to make big differences. I talked about my idea constantly, casting out for interested takers, but it wasn't until I was in Cleveland, Ohio that I met my co-founder, Catherine Hackney, PhD.

We met for lunch to put our heads and hearts together and come up with a plan for a global and a national project. As it turned out, our answers to the questions, *where would you like to have an impact, what challenge are you interested in taking on, and who do you want to work with* were all the same. For our global work, the continent that called us was Africa, being the homeland of our human ancestors and the continent where consciousness first awakened. We wanted to work with village women and children, and the issues we cared most about were education and clean water.

When we pondered our next move, we waited for direction from the universe and within one week it came— from a Dominican sister who has lived in Nigeria for 37 years, directing a non-governmental organization (NGO) in Kaduna that works with people in twenty villages developing schools, wells, and health programs. It is called Hope for the Village Child (HFVC). She invited us to come and stay with her, to do a weekend leadership training with her community, and then to visit the villages with her staff.

We visited several villages and found four room schoolhouses in every village with lots of children but few teachers. It turns out that many of the teachers live in towns or cities that are hours away. But the roads are so bad they need four wheel drive vehicles or motorcycles. So frequently they simply don't show up. When we pulled into one schoolyard in the HFVC Jeep, dozens of children came running up to us pleading, "Will you be our teacher? Will you be our teacher?" Although they had classrooms, there were no books, no tablets, no pencils or pens, and only rarely a blackboard on the wall. *This* is the image that broke my heart and led to my conviction to be of use.

After speaking with the staff and director of HFVC, Cathy and I decided to focus on the educational needs of the children, to raise money for a house for four teachers in each village, so they can live by the schools all week and go back to town on weekends. After two weeks, we came home, started the Livingkindness Foundation, put an appeal out to our communities for books, and sent over 800 children's books to the village kids in Nigeria.

We are now on our way to raising $500,000 which will fund all the teachers' housing in the 20 villages. The villagers themselves will make the bricks, construct the buildings and make all the decisions that affect their communities. It is our hope that Livingkindness can send students from the US to help with construction and build enduring bridges between our countries and our youth.

And for our local reach, we are organizing Evolutionary Creativity Olympics for teens and creating forums for the voices of GLBT youth to be heard and honored. We are also establishing chapters across the United States for people to collaborate on grassroots philanthropy projects that are evolutionary and creative. Though the foundation is still in its infant stage, it is unfolding beautifully and building a momentum that will rock the world.

This is what we are capable of. This is what can happen when we tune into our dreams, respond to our intuitions, ask ourselves what would *really* make us happy if we could do anything. When we drop the illusions of separateness that obscure our connectedness, the transcendent dimensions of our lives begin to emerge.

It is like the day when a child first discovers how to make meaning from words. Suddenly a whole new world erupts as each letter is perceived, not as a singular thing, but as an important part of a whole thought. Perhaps each of us is a letter, the world is a word, the universe is a sentence, and God is the meaning. Until we each fully manifest our letterhood, the meaning will be hidden, like the butter in cream.

When 2 irreconcilable matrices of thought and experience coincide in the mind, the result is religious or scientific breakthrough. Arthur Koestler

One child asks another, "Are you Presbyterian?
"No, we belong to another abomination."

Questions

Questions spark a conversation,
unlock cellar doors,
climb the creaky attic steps and open old trunks.

Questions are hand-written invitations,
brand new welcome mats,
door prizes and happy to see you hugs.

Questions are our favorite teachers,
the guides in the forest,
the gurus sitting in our inner chamber.

They ask, care, knock, open.
They are maps to undiscovered gold mines.

Question marks are the tools
of Solomon, Socrates, Sojourner Truth.

Don't give me a period, to stop me
an exclamation point, to shock me
a comma to justify your run-on rants
a colon to put me on hold
waiting for your list.

Don't put a parenthesis around your tender spots
and keep them from me.

Don't text me what you know.
It's already past.

Give me a question mark
so I can discover what I never
knew before.

But then again…I don't know.

What do *you* think?

VESPERS (SUNSET)

How can I get beyond duality when everywhere I look
I see something I despise?
Practice finding the One in the many,
the calm in the eye of every storm.

Having been raised a Roman Catholic, I found the concept of the "sacred feminine" to be an alien one. But one day I visited a Unity Church, and the minister led the congregation in a guided meditation where we imagined ourselves in the arms of God. There was music playing, a soft breeze was blowing through the open windows, and the minister had us imaging God's warmth and light, God's forgiveness, God's gentle mercy entering into our hearts and our whole beings. "Feel the tenderness and strength of God supporting you… Feel God's light entering into you, illuminating your very essence… Feel God's breath on you… Feel the safety of being in Her arms." At that moment, my whole body trembled. She said "Her." She called God "Her."

This was a minister in a Christian church, not some pagan at a solstice ritual. A rush of exhilaration surged through me. It was the first time in my life I'd imagined God as a woman, and in some mysterious way, I felt closer to God in that moment than ever before. It was suddenly believable that I was made in the image of God. I didn't have to try and fit into a pattern that wasn't right. This was a perfect fit. And on that day I walked out of some kind of prison.

I want to concentrate on the Holy one
melt into the fire
fuse myself to the Force of It All
but instead I chatter like the birds
sounding out my joy
chirping out my adoration
yakety-yakking for the sheer delight
of being all alone
for this sweet hour
with the love of my life.

In the measure that the soul can separate itself from multiplicity, to that extent it reveals within itself the kingdom of God. Here the soul and the Godhead are one…the whole scattered world of lower things is gathered up to oneness when the soul climbs up to that life in which there are no opposites.

Meister Eckhart

COMPLINE (9:00 PM)

What does it mean to live in oneness?
How will my life change if I do?
Your anger will turn to compassion,
your wonder will bloom into bliss.

Elephants in Mourning

Trumpeting and shrill cries of elephants in mourning were heard along a rail track in India's Assam state as a herd gathered to grieve the deaths of seven other pachyderms mowed down by a train. It was a sight to be seen rather than told. About a hundred elephants were circling the pachyderms that lay dead near the railway tracks, with tears rolling down their eyes," said Khagen Sangmal, a top official of the Digboi police station.

The Indo-Asian News Service reported that an intercity passenger train was derailed on November 15 with the engine ramming against a small herd squatting on the tracks. "No sooner the accident took place than a herd of about 100 elephants came from nowhere and were behaving like human beings mourning the deaths of dear ones. It brought tears to the eyes of the policemen and villagers," said Rantu Das, another police official.

My Soul Speaks to My Body on Its Deathbed

It never mattered how you looked
the $65 haircut
the leather boots from Nordstrom's
even the Honda hybrid wasn't that important
What mattered was the night you said
in front of everyone

I'm sorry to that student you'd hurt

It didn't matter that you got standing ovations,
were popular on Facebook and had a few good reviews
What mattered is that you every time you spoke
you told the truth, opened your heart,
dared to cry and laugh out loud.

It didn't matter that you couldn't find an agent,
or a partner, or that handyman you wished for
What mattered is that, as alone as you were,
you kept on working, kept on writing,
kept a comforter handy for the ones needing warmth.

It didn't matter that you let the phone ring,
spent that whole day in bed, took naps
in the daytime to rest your brain
What mattered were those $20 bills you mailed out
to your high school English teacher who lives alone,
those groceries and meals you carried up
to your mother's apartment,
that phone call to your brother offering to come
for the weekend and help him clean out his garage.

It didn't matter that you had a house in the east
and a house in the west,
that you had gorgeous scarves
and jaw-dropping photos on all your walls
What mattered is the dinner parties you had
that brought people together,
made a sacrament of the sound of their words
falling like leaves into the soil of another.

It never mattered that you fell over drunk
from Margaritas, that you traded your body

for a bed off the highway that night you hitchhiked
from Berkeley to Oregon,
that you smoked or snorted whatever you did
before you woke up to a brighter day.
What mattered was that you wrangled conversations
like a rodeo superstar,
transformed lamentations into illuminations,
converted noise and static into sonnets and sonatas.

It didn't matter that you never learned yoga,
didn't exercise like you said you would,
spent whole days in the toyshop of your office
turning nothing into something
that would matter to someone.
It mattered that you had forgiven everyone,
and realized finally there was nothing to forgive.

It matters that you came out,
stood out, spoke out, sang out,
acted out and broke out
before you wore out.

And as you prepare to return to the Mother
it matters now, that your light will go on
to feed the living as your body
feeds the soil where you are laid to rest.

The trees, upon seeing the ax come into the forest, notice its wooden handle and say, "Look, one of us." Hassidic saying

What question is in your mind? Get clear about it and ask it every day. Ask the trees, the river, the North Star, your co-worker, your neighbor. The universe is supporting you in every way, but you have to become transparent to it. You have to reveal yourself. The universe will provide, but only after you say what you need. What is it you need? What are you looking for?

Sunday morning at my Mom's

I let her sleep while I do my morning prayers and make an altar on the coffee table. I place photos of our loved ones on the altar—some who have died, some who are living. I fill a small pitcher with water and put two bowls and a hand towel next to it on the table. I find the Jerusalem Bible for one reading, and a copy of Making Peace, my own book, for the second reading. I bring two glasses half-filled with the only juice she has, a nice white grape peach, and put a slice of Canadian Oat bread on a plate.

I take one of the paintings that she painted and a photograph of mine off the wall and put them on the altar—symbols of our creativity to remind us that we are continuing the creation through the work of our hands. I place a small bottle of frankincense oil next to the water. I open her violin case and place it on the couch where she'll be sitting. I put Beth Nielsen Chapman's *Hymns* in the CD player, light the candle, then go to wake her.

"Time for church, Mom, Wake up!"

She rolls over, opens her arms and I crawl into her bed and give her a big hug. Then she puts on her warm robe and slippersocks that she made herself, grabs her walker, makes a pit stop in the bathroom, and heads for the living room to take her place on the couch. I hand her a cup of coffee and we review what the morning ritual is going to look like.

She agrees to play the opening song and decides on the *Queen of Hearts* waltz. She picks up the fiddle and bow and begins our ritual. Then we have our two readings, and after each we talk about what they meant to us, what came to mind and what was stirred inside by them. This takes about twenty minutes, then we share for a bit about where we fell short of our own standards and expectations during the week.

I start the *Hymns* CD and begin the ceremony of blessing the water. I pour water into each of the bowls and we dip our fingers into the bowls and send the energy of our purest love and compassion into the water. Once blessed, we pour the water from both our bowls back into the pitcher. Next we come to the blessing of the hands, where we wash our hands of guilt and regret and resolve to be more mindful in the week to come. I pour water over her hands and offer her the towel, then she does the same for me as I absolve myself. *Panis Angeli-cus* is playing in the background

After that, imagining the ever presence of the ones in the photos, we pick up the frames one by one and express the feelings we have toward each person. On this morning, we speak to my Dad, my Uncle Paul, and Mom's three sis-ters—Margaret Rose, Kay and Ruth. This takes some time, as there are many feelings to be expressed that have never been spoken. Tears of joy and sorrow co-mingle on our faces. After that, Mom plays *You Are My Sunshine* and I sing along.

Next, we share stories of how we offer ourselves to the world, what we do consciously to live out our prayers and our commitments. At the end, I play *You Are the River, I am the Flow* from my CD and we reflect on ourselves as the body of God, the hands and eyes and ears of God. Then, to expand our imagi-nations, we take a few minutes to imagine what our spirituality would look like if we were raised as a peasant girl in China, brought up without a particular no-tion of God. At the end, Mom writes this reflection:

I am small. My mother feeds me, holds me, takes care of me.
I don't want to be away from her.
I am ten. My brothers and sisters watch over me.
I want to be with them.
My father is kind and takes care that we have food.
This feeling I have is what?
Love, caring...

From this place of union, we begin our communion, remembering how it might have been at the supper when Jesus tried to say to the disciples, "Don't forget how important this is: to share bread and wine, to come together in body, mind and spirit, to fortify yourselves for the work of compassion and peacemaking." *Adoramus Te* plays in the background while Mom and I eat our bread and drink our juice. When we're finished, she plays an old fiddle tune from her father called *Deedle De De.*

I pick up the bottle of oil, put some frankincense on my fingertip and rub it into the space between her eyes, "That you might have vision, Mom, to see where you are needed, and power to heal and soothe the wounds of others; and that light might continue to enter into you and guide your steps as you journey forward." Then she anoints me and the morning ritual is complete. We end with *Amazing Grace,* then I pour our holy water into a jar and put it in her bedside stand.

CHAPTER SIX SATURDAY

Do what you want. That's not selfish. What's selfish is expecting other people to do what you want. Anthony de Mello (1931-1987)

JOY AND DESIRE

A s I sit down to write this chapter on joy today, I realize it is the first anniversary of Haiti's earthquake. When it occurred, I was on my way to a Dominican Retreat Center in Ossining, New York. I was to facilitate planning days for the religious community's leadership team and two weekend workshops for leadership development and mission promotion. It was a Tuesday.

On Wednesday at lunch, Sr. Bette Ann Jaster, who had recently moved to New York to be on the Leadership Team, asked the question, "What can we do for Haiti? They didn't have a choice and we don't either. It has to be soon. How about a concert with Pete Seeger? We could call it Hope for Haiti." Pete was one of Bette Ann's long time heroes. She had been an activist all her life and had just left her job of working with the homeless in Denver. Seeing the images of all the people left homeless in Haiti touched a nerve in her.

Someone asked "Do you know him?"

"He lives just up the river in Beacon and I know him from the Ribbon Project, the Shad festival and his music. I know he'll do it if he can," said Bette Ann.

 Pass the cookies please," came the response.

"When and where would we have it?" asked another.

"In the chapel this Sunday," said Bette Ann.

"He's 90 some years old," said another, with a kind of *it'll never happen* tone. Nobody else picked up on the idea. We finished our cookies and headed off for the meeting room to resume our visioning. On the way there, I started to get excited about Bette Ann's idea. It was an extraordinary vision. Why not go for it, even if it *was* a long shot? I called Syracuse Cultural Workers, an arts for social justice organization I'd co-founded in the 80s, knowing they'd have Pete's personal phone number. They did. I wrote it down and walked into the meeting room.

"I've got Pete's phone number," I said, handing it over to Bette Ann. She left the room to make the call.

In five minutes Bette Ann walked in the room with a big smile on her face. Pete had agreed to do a benefit concert on Sunday afternoon. That gave us 3 days to get the word out, in the midst of all our other agendas. The leadership team gave Bette Ann the afternoon to work up the publicity materials and to put the PR campaign into action with the help of the retreat center staff. By Thursday morning we were back to our sessions with Bette Ann back in the circle.

We had a day long workshop on Saturday, and another full day on Sunday which ended at 3 pm. By 5 pm, I was backstage tuning up with Pete Seeger, Tom Chapin and Michael Mark who had also volunteered their talents. Come to find out, Bette Ann had included my name in the press release, listing me as a singer-songwriter who'd also be performing. This was going to be some night!

On a cold, icy evening in the great Northeast, 600 people came out to the Dominican Retreat Center and donated over $19,000 for the people of Haiti. Last I heard, that figure was up to $26,000. And it all started with one woman asking one question: *why not?* This was her heart's desire—to reach out together to Haiti with Pete Seeger and her friends and neighbors, to sing and pray and contribute to her sisters and brothers in need. It was fun, it was an act of faith, and it was fruitful—all the earmarks of evolutionary creativity.

Studying the mystics from medieval times, one would think that joy is not a way station on the spiritual path. Catherine of Siena is said to have brought crying to new decibel levels. Teresa of Avila, John of the Cross, Hildegarde of Bingen, Julian of Norwich, each of them and many more sought to deepen their intimacy with God through self-sacrifice and suffering. As if the more it hurts, the closer I must be getting to God.

But these days, at least through the lens of this creator, it seems that the more joyful it is, the more it feels divinely inspired. I do not subscribe to the notion that we should eliminate desire from our life—that desire lies at the root of suffering, as the Buddhists hold it, or that desire as a human emotion should be stifled before it advances into something sinful which is more a Christian perspective.

Desire is the beginning of life. Desire is the yearning of every particle to extend its experience by fusing with its opposite. Our visions are born from our desires; our evolution is fueled by our desires. Through desire and emotion we create movement, which creates change, which excites and expands consciousness. The question should always be: what is my heart's desire? If you are conscious enough to be thinking of evolving yourself forward, you are conscious enough to trust that your heart's desire will be something that is as good for others as it is for you.

Mysticism always leads to the transcendence of all limits. Leonardo Boff

MATINS (MIDNIGHT)

My desire is deep and enduring
You are here and yet do I yearn
To see you, Beloved, to feel you,
O would my heart turn to fire.

It is the gift of our essence that attracts others to our light. It is our speaking out that calls forth the one we seek. Just as the beauty of a rose summons the bee when it is time for pollination, or the flickering flame charms the moth, so does the brilliance of our soul draw others toward us when we dare to bare it. There is nothing more luminous and alluring than the human soul revealing itself.

I come alive in your presence when you speak your truths. I come alive when you ask your questions, cry your tears, stutter out your anxieties and terrors. I come alive because I find myself in your brokenness. I feel every bone in my body when I walk with you through the ruins of your life. When I am there with you on the perilous edge, there is hope for the two of us. We are not alone then and we know it. Underneath that rubble of sorrow and loss, like a seed breaking open and moving for the first time of its own accord, so do we break open and make our way steadily toward the light.

While it once seemed there was a "you" and a "me," we now understand there is only one of us. And while it once appeared that one was giving as the other received, we know now that giving *is* receiving.

Longing

I am the alms looking for the orphan
I am the blanket searching for the cold
I am the cure looking for the healer
I am the diamond longing for the coal.

I am an ending seeking the beginning,
I am feeling pining after form,
I am the gallows calling to forgiveness

I am a haven longing for the storm.

I am the inner calling for the outer
I am a jewel crying for the mine
I am kinship searching for a family
I am the light-year hungering for time.

I am midnight chasing after morning,
I am newness aching for the old
I am oneness calling for the many
I am passion looking for a soul.

I am the question longing for the seeker,
I am the rainbow yearning for the rain,
I am solace looking for the mourner
I am triumph thirsting after pain.

I am union calling to the lonely
I am the voyage looking for the way
I am the wind longing for the windmill
I am the yin falling for the yang.

As the spirit sings out for a body,
And the body ones itself to soul
I am ever fused to the Beloved
I am the part bowing to the Whole.

LAUDS (SUNRISE)

I feel you in my bedroom,
in my office and kitchen as well
There is nowhere to go to avoid you
for it's in my breath that you dwell.

Most people, when asked what worldly possessions they would try to save if their house was on fire, mention photographs immediately. "I could replace everything else but my pictures," they say. "They're the most precious possessions I have. My whole life is in those photo albums."

Photographs provide evidence of our lives having meant something. They show our relationships with people, the places we've traveled to, the events we've celebrated and honored. Of all the things that happen to us in the course of our lives, those which are most important get photographed, filed, put into books and albums that we leave behind like legacies. They're our own form of autobiography, a telling of the tale of who we are.

I once visited a woman in Germany who had created a photo album for each of her four children. It was not a collection of haphazard snapshots edited together out of a huge shoebox stash in the closet, but a carefully conceived and laid out work of art. Each album was a beautifully bound leather book and every photograph in it was perfectly composed, elegantly lit, dramatically designed, and placed on the page with lush amounts of white space.

She never referred to herself as a photographer, but these were some of the most touching portraits I had ever seen, all taken from family vacations, summer trips to the mountains, weekend excursions in the Volkswagen van. She was making art of their family rituals—an act that called for nothing more than attention and love.

In the course of our lives we are all witness to events that honor the passages, the triumphs and tragedies of human existence. Whether these be moments of birth, death, communal gatherings, revolutions, rallies, or family reunions, they are events that signify and symbolize our connection with each other, our commitment to something bigger than ourselves. These rituals are what keep us bonded, buoyant in the face of turbulence, bound together in spirit when our journeys move us apart.

150

Years ago, I went to photograph my mother competing in the Senior Games. Her events were over by mid-morning and though I had planned to leave when she was done competing, the atmosphere at the Games was so magnetic I couldn't tear myself away. There was more life, more vigor and joy and kinship there than I had witnessed in a long time.

I was standing next to a woman photographing the pole vault event, watching 80-85 year old men hurl their lean bodies over a bar six feet high. Both of us had our cameras glued to our faces, and when she lowered hers to reload film, tears were streaming down her cheeks. "I've never been so emotional in my life," she said. "This is the most touching experience I've ever had, the most beautiful thing I've ever photographed."

A 71 year old from Pennsylvania was warming up on the sidelines, bending, testing and checking his pole. "When I read about the pole event, I realized there wasn't much competition so I decided to take it up. My kids were ready to beat me up when I came home with a pole one day, but it's been a great sport to compete in. I race-walk, too. Used to be I could win it going backward, but now there's so many competitors, I never win, but I keep on trying."

Another pole vaulter, an 80 year old, admitted he was jittery about the event. The week before he had collided with someone in volleyball and still had a few stitches in his forehead. He was so nervous about hitting the bar that, when his turn came, he soared over it like a flying gymnast, with several feet between his body and the bar. "I used to think I ought to give it up," he said, "until I watched a man with a prosthetic leg in the race-walking event. He struggled and struggled around that track, his face full of pain, his legs wobbling under the pressure. He was the last to come in, but everyone was cheering him on, and when he crossed the finish line, the crowd roared like I'll never forget. Ever since then, I'm committed to these Games."

As I walked around the track's infield, photographing competitors warming up and stretching, taping their javelins, checking their times, wrapping their ankles, I was caught off guard by the emotions that surfaced. There was something magical, something almost holy about being in the presence of 5000 elders who were risking and reaching beyond the norm, passing their courage like a baton to anyone in the relay ready to take it.

In the way that the spirit is uplifted by music, transformed by art, calmed by prayer, it is also empowered by collective endeavor. And it was the endeavor, the enthusiasm and earnestness of these athletes that touched me so deeply.

After watching the women's long jump for 75-80 year olds, I walked up to the competitors who were congratulating each other for a fine performance. I meant to ask them how it felt to be Senior Olympians, but when my lip started to quiver, I asked, "Why do these events make me cry?"

A jumper who had just won a silver for second place said, "You're looking deep into the future here, and watching all of us do this lets you know that you will be able to do this too, and your kids will be able to do this, and their kids. We're passing on a dream, a possibility, a kind of hope for the future—isn't that worth a tear or two?"

These are the kinds of ceremonies and rituals that heal us in the beholding. Joy arises when we're part of something grand and communal. For us to see images that reveal our collective love for life, images of people stretching their limits, contributing what they have to the common good—this is a gift for the eyes and soul.

Haven't we seen enough pictures of war horrors, Hollywood celebrities, dysfunctional families? Isn't it time to add our own images to the archives of history, to tell our version of life as it unfolded before our eyes?

PRIME (6:00 A.M.)

I call to you morning and evening
only your name on my lips
my windows and doors are all open
in my heart is a throne made of gold.

When I was a sophomore in high school, I had a homeroom teacher who turned my life upside down. While all the other nuns were busy trying to get us not to act like teenagers, not to give vent to our boisterous energy and passion, Sister Robert Joseph did the opposite. She had us express it, get into it and see where it took us. In every other classroom, we started class by standing up at our desks and reciting a prayer. In her classroom, we started by reciting poetry. In the beginning of the semester, she handed out a mimeographed sheet of five poems. The poets included e.e.cummings, Emily Dickinson, Elizabeth Barrett

Browning, Christina Rosetti, and Gerard Manley Hopkins.

When the bell rang, we stood up, and each day recited a different poem from the sheet. Within weeks, we no longer needed those papers. We were reciting from memory.

From e.e.cummings,

i thank You God for most this amazing
day: for the leaping greenly spirits of trees
and a blue true dream of sky; and for everything
which is natural which is infinite which is yes

From Elizabeth Barrett Browning,

All are not taken; there are left behind
Living Belovèds, tender looks to bring
And make the daylight still a happy thing,
And tender voices, to make soft the wind…

From Emily Dickinson,

Had I not seen the Sun
I could have borne the shade
But Light a newer Wilderness
My Wilderness has made –

Some days we would take a poem and spend the hour discussing it, or writing about it, or writing our own poems based on its style. Or we would write essays on things that mattered in our lives, and she would draw out our passion, try and get at what was going on inside of us so that our writing would be alive and meaningful to us.

In my entire life, no one had dared to stimulate that kind of thinking or writing. All the adults, it seemed, wanted to stifle it. Here we were, fifteen, sixteen years old, in the midst of some of the biggest changes our bodies would be going through, carrying around the biggest questions we had ever asked as we edged closer to the world of maturity, and she was the only one asking us to express these things. The only one willing to talk about the conflicts we were meeting heart and head on.

Until that year, every attempt was made to shape us into a certain mold. Be this way. Think this way. Deny these feelings. Follow these rules. We were being led like sheep to do the right thing which was always presented to us with no room for discussion, no allowance for who we were in the matter or what we thought.

What Sister Robert Joseph did differently was to invite us, to insist really, on us forming our own conscience about what was going on in our lives. She used literature and poetry to engage us, to bring up the subjects and she had us expand on them in whatever way felt true to us. No criticism of our thoughts, only our tentativeness. What she called forth was the courage to think for ourselves, to explore inside ourselves and see what WE thought.

By bringing up the big questions in life that literature and poetry addressed, she was helping us shape our future. Helping us see what we loved most, what called us to action, what we would stand for, live for, insist upon in our own lives. She released us from bondage to the black and white thinking we had been exposed to all our lives. Her respect for our thoughts and passions gave us permission to think and feel deeply. When she went to march in Selma, Alabama with Martin Luther King, Jr., we understood more clearly what it meant to have a commitment and act on it. When we organized a student strike against the suspension of one of our classmates, she stood in the window with her fist raised and went to the principal in support of our action. It was not her words that taught us, it was her actions, the respect she gave us, the way she guided us to our own inner knowing.

What happened in that classroom was a rite of initiation, an invitation to claim our own opinions and shape our own lives. For me, it was a launching into another dimension, an untethering of sorts that freed me to float toward a future I had not yet imagined—a future I would create from those passions she unearthed.

Christmas Day Thoughts from a Brooding Post-Christian

No savior born this day
No need to be saved
No sin on the soul
No Adam and Eve in the garden
No talking snake and voice in the sky
No Virgin Mary
No donkey ride to Bethlehem
No rejection at the inn
No wise men with gifts
Just one good story
That's lasted 2000 years
And not much different
from the tales told 2000 years before that.

We are not the same tribespeople,
the same nomads and villagers
who would believe anything they were told.
We go for the provable
the well-researched
the steeped in truth tales of wonder and awe.

No raising of the dead,
water into wine,
walking on water for us.

He was one of us, he said.
Whatever he did, we can do
he said.

I have my own story.
It doesn't matter.
There's no right or wrong here.
It was 2000 years ago and no one was taking notes.

Jesus was born one of seven.
His mother was no virgin.
He worked some with wood,
but more with his mind.
He thought new thoughts.
Opened himself to revelation
Told stories day and night
Was a vessel of the new
Stood for justice, taught forgiveness
Crucified for not caving in.

That's the miracle of Jesus if there is one
He thought his own thoughts
when no one else did.
Dangerous. But he never stopped.
That's what I celebrate today.
His original thinking.
O holy night.

TERCE (9:00 A.M.)

O Holy Earth! cries the human.
O Holy Sun! cries the earth.
O Holy Sky! cries the sun.
O Holy Galaxies! cries the sky.
O Holy Light! cries the galaxies.
O Holy Dark! cries the Light.

Stop learning. Start knowing. Rumi

When you highlight something as you read, or underline a passage, you're giving a little standing ovation to the author. You're applauding how nicely they described something you already knew. You're registering your resonance with their elegance of expression. Every atom in your body has been around for 14 billion years. Left alone, your bodymind is brilliant. There's nothing you don't already know.

What keeps us from acting that way, or thinking that way, are all the filters we have in place—religious filters, cultural filters, race filters, gender filters. We're exposed to hundreds of ads a day designed to make us feel insecure, anxious, inadequate so we'll buy the products they're selling to cure us. Ten years ago The Dallas Morning News reported that we each see more ads in one year than people 50 years ago saw in their entire lifetime. Imagine how that's increased in a decade.

So how do we immunize ourselves against the toxins that come at us every waking hour? How do we remove the filters from our lens and see the unadulterated light? If it's true we're hardwired for bliss, how do we fix our corrupt software?

We've been programmed for consumption, but as educator Paulo Freire reminds us, "We may be conditioned, but we're not determined." Any one of us can override the prejudices, opinions and programming that we've been subjected to all our lives. And the good news is: the process of enlightenment is a process of subtraction, not addition, according to mystic Meister Eckhart. All the intelligence of the cosmos is in our cellular makeup. The question is not what more do we have to learn, but what illusions do we have to let go of?

When Einstein talked about the optical delusion of consciousness, he was referring to our tendency to think of our selves, our feelings and thoughts as separate from the rest of humanity. He likened this limited thinking to a prison and suggested our only way out was to expand our circle of compassion to the earth itself and all its creatures. And what are the odds of anyone succeeding in this who is barraged all day with news that capitalizes on our differences?

It takes a commitment and a high level of spiritual intelligence to maintain a consciousness of global communion. It is counter-cultural, but not counter-intuitive. We have evolved from bacteria that survived because it adapted to changing environments, collaborated with neighboring strains, contributed what DNA they didn't need to a common gene library and evolved themselves into collectives of nucleated cells *of which we ourselves are composed.* Evolution biologist Dr. Elisabet Sahtouris, in her book *Manifesto for Change: Crisis as Opportunity* writes: "Eventually, in their encounters with each other, archebacteria somehow discovered the advantages of cooperation over competition: that feeding our enemy is more energy efficient (read: less costly) than killing them off." She concludes that the sustainability of any entity depends on its coming into harmony with whatever surrounds it in a mutual give and take that makes it more or less indispensable to the whole in which it is embedded.

This is the economic system the earth has arrived at after four billion years of experience. And that's why it would be smart to stop asking *What Would Jesus Do?* and start asking *What Would Nature Do?* We *are* nature. We are earth evolving itself through us. It is all one Intelligence, coursing through the rivers, coursing through the redwoods, coursing through our bloodstreams and brain cells. The very same Intelligence that triggers the first heartbeat in a human embryo has kept this planet rotating and revolving and evolving for billions of years. Our solutions are already embedded in the atoms within and around us. We are not lacking in answers. We are lacking in kindness, in imagination, in soul force.

When I underlined these words of Dr. Sahtouris, I did it because they made my cells shiver with delight, my heart leap a little in its chest cavity. They filled me with awe and joy, as if all the cells inside me were saying "Yes! Yes! Pass this on! Spread some GOOD news around for a change!" So here's her image to delight in:

"Consider that the DNA that codes for the proteins of which you are largely made is stuffed into the nucleus of each of your invisibly small cells in a two-meter length, along with some protein and water. As you contain some fifty trillion or more cells, putting these two meter lengths end to end, your DNA would reach so far into space that a jet pilot flying day and night would be flying well over ten thousand years to reach the end of your personal DNA string." That's looking at things sub-atomically.

Looking at things biologically gives us another awe-inspiring view. Except for hydrogen, which is 1/10th our weight, our body is pure stardust. Even though water consists of two hydrogen atoms for every oxygen atom, hydrogen has much less mass. So we can estimate that 93% of the mass in our body is stardust. Whomever you are right now, what comprises your body was once a burning star in outer space.

The iron atoms in your blood that are delivering oxygen to your cells came from exploding white dwarf stars, according to Joel Primack and Nancy Abrams who co-authored *The View from the Center of the Universe*. The oxygen you breathe comes from exploding supernovas that ended the lives of massive stars, and the carbon you exhale is from planetary nebulas, death clouds of middle size stars slightly larger than our sun.

Ten years ago, what we knew from space led us to calculate that there was one galaxy per person in the universe. Now, thanks to the Hubble telescope, calculations have been adjusted and it seems there are 125 billion galaxies in the universe. We're now up to 18 galaxies per person. And recently a German supercomputer simulation put that number even higher, at 500 billion. In other words, there could be a galaxy out there for every star in the Milky Way. According to one science buff's calculations, at one galaxy per second, it could take just short of four thousand years to count all the galaxies in the universe.

The cosmology I grew up with never sparked the awe that these ideas spark. There are hundreds of creation stories from hundreds of different cultures, and each one provides a framework for the collective consciousness of that culture. When science and religion were torn asunder in the Middle Ages, the Christian cosmology we inherited gave us an image of an All-Powerful Father God who pulled strings and made things happen from his throne in heaven. An appreciation for the sacredness of our own beings was not passed down. An appreciation for our role as co-creators was not passed down. Nor was an appreciation for the sacredness of the Feminine, the sacredness of the Earth, and the mysterious, sacred splendor of the cosmos.

A cosmological filter was put in place and put a limit on our imagination. Galileo was imprisoned as a heretic in 1633 for saying that the sun, not the earth, was the center of the universe, and the Church has continued to this day to silence thought leaders and activists who rally to the beat of another drum, doing the very things Jesus did in his day—speak truth to power and truth *from* power. This is, indeed, no ordinary time, as spiritual evolutionaries and cultural creatives begin to merge in body, mind, and spirit.

Consciousness is rising like cream as people evolve themselves forward as planetary co-creators, modern-day mystics and contemporary prophets. We are falling in love with our earth again, communing with the Divine that lives within, opening our imaginations to the possibility of ending hunger, ending war, dissolving imaginary and real borders, and extending education to every child. Paul Hawken, in his inspiring book *Blessed Unrest*, refers to the millions of individuals and organizations reaching out across the planet to work toward common goals in the most uncommon and imaginative ways. He calls it the largest social movement in history without a name and his message is one of pure hope and joy.

We are doing it. We are committed. We are speaking out. We are leaving our churches if we have to, to speak out for justice, for equanimity, for kindness. Evolutionary creators are not waiting for governments, not waiting for business, not waiting for religions to catch up and get it right. We are doing our work every minute of the day—maintaining our spiritual practice, honoring our bodies, creating the world we want to be in with our thoughts, our words, our actions. Life is happening *through* us, not to us. And though there are unpredictable, chaotic, meteoric events we are called upon to respond to, it is more a cosmic dance than anything — a chance to practice unity consciousness, stay mindful, remain calm and rooted in joy.

SEXT (NOON)

You enter me like a wavelength
quiet as a desert at night
you become my thoughts and movements
my life is You turned inside out.

Of all the metaphors for human life unfolding toward its highest goal, the metaphor of the journey seems most apt. Even if what we feel we are moving toward exists already within us, even if the movement toward wholeness occurs solely in our own consciousness, getting there is nevertheless a journey of epic proportions—no less dangerous, fearful, and perilous than a journey through the darkest, demon-ridden forest.

As the collective human myth tells it, we must all travel from the dark to the light, pass through fire, choose nobly, act heroically, and prove ourselves worthy of good reputation in this life and just rewards in the next. And though many have the insight that that the "heaven" we are leaning toward is the precious life we already have, until that knowing reaches critical mass and runs through the consciousness of all, we will continue to speak as if we are separate from others and the God we seek. Hence the journey *toward*, the metaphor of passage, of progress, of movement forward.

The ritual of pilgrimage is dense with meaning. To make a pilgrimage is a courageous act, a leave-taking from the common circumstances of our lives to unknown paths ahead. The point is rarely what we find at the end of the journey, but what happens to us as we trudge along, wayfarers in the night, wanderers in pursuit of the Holy Grail.

A few years ago I took part in such a pilgrimage, traveling to Iceland with seventeen women writers from the United States and Canada. Before I went, it had never occurred to me that, like the human body, the Earth has energy centers similar to the chakras of Hindu thought, power spots that can be visited and experienced. When I registered for the trip, billed as a journey to the Earth's heart chakra, I had my doubts about the whole chakra thing, but I suspended them for the chance to experience such an exotic event.

Arriving in Iceland, few of us could say why we were there, though most acknowledged that we had made the trip in response to a voice from within that wouldn't be silenced. Our guides were Sunneva and Hildur, both psychics with the ability to see energy fields and colors emanating from the land masses around them. Sunneva had grown up on Iceland's Snaefellsnes Peninsula and was familiar with all of the enchanted spots in the area.

On the way to the glacier, Hildur told us stories about the strong women of Nordic sagas and the giantesses who live in the cone-shaped mountains. We stopped at sites along the way where, we were assured, the energy was power-ful and the unseen (by me) colors brilliant. "Here there are great waves of en-ergy. You can pick stones that will help you on your journey, some from the lava rocks and some from the pebble beach. They have different qualities and can be used for different things," we were told.

We climbed up red hills of lava, sinking into the ash that blanketed the craters. We walked on carpets of lichen-covered rocks, through blossoming heaths toward the delft blue sea where the dragon rocks lay. We drank from the waters of a sacred spring, marked by a statue of the Blessed Mother. Sunneva and Hildur led us through centers of male and female energy, past statues to the gods and into grottoes of the goddesses. We snaked along the cliffs in a long line of color, our hiking clothes bright against the pale blue sky.

It was high summer, the season of the midnight sun, and darkness never in-truded into the night. Each evening at midnight, we formed a circle, shared sto-ries from the day, and sent our spirits into the heart of the glacier. I often ventured out into the pale gray night, photographing the silhouettes of cattle and craters, listening to the night birds and the gentle winds.

All along the way, we plagued our guides with questions about the heart chakra. How would we know when we got there? What *happens* at the heart chakra? Would we feel different vibrations when we got there? Was it like our bodies' heart chakra? Were we almost there? How can we tell when we get close? We were like a bunch of tourists trying so hard to get to our destination we almost missed the journey.

Sunneva and Hildur were patient with us, though their answer to most of our questions was little more than a smile. When we finally arrived at the base of the glacier, we followed Sunneva to a sparkling blue stream. The stream, she said, was a source of power, for it ran from the glacier southward, along the ley line that aligned Snaefellsjokul with Glastonbury, Stonehenge, and the pyra-mids of Giza. I sat quietly, squinting into the snow-covered mountain, surrounded by the others who had sat down in a circle around Sunneva.

With the wind gently blowing her red hair and a handful of heather in her palm, Sunneva spoke to us about the journey we were ending. She explained how it was determined that the glacier held the heart chakra for the planet and why she hadn't been willing to answer our many questions about body chakras and Earth chakras.

"In the East and in the West," she said, "the mind is an important part of spiritual discipline. Whether one is engaged in emptying it or filling it up, the mind is primary in Eastern and Western spiritual experience. In the North, on the other hand, we find our spiritual power in Nature. To us, spiritual wisdom cannot be taught, only *experienced*. It is not something we think of, but something we feel. And we feel it *with* the earth and *in* the earth. You had to walk these paths, hear these birds, climb these hills in order to take in the power of the North, in order to feel the energy of this glacier. And now you have it in you. It is yours forever."

Sunneva then left the circle and knelt down to drink from the stream. Others followed, sipping the crystal blue water from the cup of their hands—the final rite of passage in our journey to the heart.

The eyes are here for seeing, but the soul is here for its own joy. Rumi

NONE (3:00 PM)

What joy is mine upon waking
I feel your presence within
I know that the air I am breathing
is the ether of the heaven I'm in.

In Japan, I was invited to speak to a group of A-bomb survivors at the Nagasaki Association for the Promotion of Peace and to present my slideshow, *Focus on Peace*. Before my presentation, the program called for us to watch the premiere of a Japanese film that included recently released American military footage of the Nagasaki bombing.

I sat in the back of the room with Mr. Matsunaga, director of the organization, who served as my translator. The lights dimmed, and the film began with a slow pan of the Nagasaki Peace Park. Paper cranes and colorful flowers filled the frame. Then a jump cut took us to the cockpit of an American warplane on August 9, 1945.

We watched the bomb drop. Watched the deadly cloud devour the city. And then from the ground we watched what followed. Mr. Matsunaga, his calm voice silenced, collapsed into tears by my side. The survivors in front of us sat still as sculptures. Frozen in time, they stared ahead, some gasping as they saw images of themselves on the screen, stumbling through the rubble of charred corpses. Dazed and burned, survivors were calling for families they would never find. Quiet sobs filled the room as we witnessed the rerun of a nuclear holocaust.

When it was over, no one moved. No one turned on a light. We sat there in the dark amidst sobs and tears. When the lights came on, and I was introduced, I stood before them and started to cry. "I'm so sorry," I said. "I'm so sorry." Tears ran down my face as I looked out into the crowd of survivors. Their eyes, too, were full of tears, but they urged me to go on.

I spoke about the slides we were going to see, with Mr. Matsunaga at my side translating. Then the lights went out again, the music started, and images of millions of people marching for peace began to dissolve into each other. There were no words in the slideshow, just the pictures and voices from the International Children's Choir singing *Let There Be Peace on Earth*. The images of colorful, festive, life-affirming demonstrations had more power that day than any I remember. Symbols of a commitment to peace washed over and comforted us. They delivered us, if only momentarily, from the fear that a nuclear holocaust might happen again, for how could these millions marching and chanting and praying for world peace *not* make a difference?

After the slideshow, the survivors came to the microphone one by one to speak of the impact the photographs had had on them: "I did not know so many people cared about what happened to us...We thought we were all alone in our struggle... Seeing that so many Americans care about peace encourages my efforts...How can we fail if there are so many of us?" After a heart-rending start, we found our joy together, made all the more poignant by the tears we'd dared to share.

We can't articulate the way art heals us anymore than we can articulate the mystery of the cosmos. We are awed by the gifts of art, soothed by its music, comforted by its imagery, inspired by its revelations of the possible and the passionate. Art speaks from the soul, to the soul. It has a language of its own. It is the language of the universe, the music of the spheres.

VESPERS (SUNSET)

Why do we seek what we already have?
why look for that which we've found?
This humanness seems so silly
we desire most that which abounds.

The reason I'm pouring my wine into this Book of Hours chalice is because I wanted a way to interrupt your thoughts. It would betray logic to have a book on evolutionary creativity come in just another old wineskin—chapter after chapter of sentences and paragraphs. It would be like standing at a podium and simply talking for an hour. No thank you. It's not my thoughts I want to share with you as much as my joy, my feelings, my soul.

And the only way I can be sure to have these drift down into your heart zone is if I use the arts to open the channel between your brain and heart. We already know it's *inspiration*, not information we need. And what inspires us? The creations of others, in any form—stories, songs, poems, images. We love to see what people are creating. It's what feeds us, sustains us, entertains us, alters us consciously, emotionally, spiritually.

I can't provide lessons on how to be a sacrament-maker, because it doesn't call for rules. It calls for courage, sensitivity, confidence, ability to risk, to be adventurous and vulnerable. It calls for spontaneity. It demands of us a willingness to evoke spirit, to speak from our depths, to name the sorrows or joys we are celebrating and say why it matters. There's nothing wrong with having priests, rabbis and ministers performing rituals. It's simply time for us to empower *ourselves* for the task, to name ourselves as bestowers of grace.

There are occasions occurring all day long that call for our attention, that are worthy of a moment's focus, if only a grace before meals. To gather a group's attention, to start a meeting with a moment of silence, a piece of music for centering, a request for assistance from the ancestors—whatever is appropriate for the occasion—these are unifying acts, gifts to the whole from the one. And once we know *why* it is important that we ordain ourselves as priests of the imagination, all the *hows* will fall into place.

Why is it important to create an altar wherever you are and honor our oneness whenever you can? Why is it important to take our power, unleash our passion, and celebrate the sacrament of self-proclamation? Why are rituals and ceremonies the thresholds to transformation, the doorways into our own divinity? Why must we learn the language of unity, and discard the words that divide and distance us?

Once we are clear that *we are the help*, we are the healers and creators of this prophetic age, then our rituals will be spontaneous, spirit-driven rites that lead people onward and forward in their lives. Every moment the spirit is whispering messages to the body: light this candle, put your hand here, play this music, read this poem, touch her head like this. We are guided every step of the way by Love Itself and when love is our only agenda, only love will unfold in our presence. And when love unfolds and penetrates a group, that event becomes sacramental—a grace-bestowing rite.

People are looking for the REAL thing. They are leaving churches in droves because it's not there. No one needs to hear what God wants, what God thinks, who's making God mad. That insults our souls. God does not have emotions. Nor has it served us for centuries to maintain the image of an actual Person on an actual throne in an actual location called heaven. This has crippled us spiritually. We have abdicated our power, denied our own divinity, refused to accept that "we are gods" as God said, if you believe in the Bible.

Our families and neighborhoods and cities and nations would benefit hugely from us taking responsibility for the creation of our lives, after the Mysterious One breathed life into our own nostrils. That we live and breathe is the miracle that launched us, but the journey to wholeness is in our hands. And because we *are* interdependent—cells in the same Body, offspring of the same ancestors, shoots from the same root—then the wellness of one is dependent on the wellness of all. The more spiritually intelligent we are, the more of the cosmos is in our view, and the better we embody heaven and earth.

Water flowing downhill is its nature.
A maple leaf changing color is its nature.
Steam evaporating into air is its nature.
A yearling maturing into a mare is its nature.
A spider weaving its web is its nature.
An icicle melting into water is its nature.

166

A pine cone growing into a pine tree is its nature.
A human dissolving into the Divine is its nature.

If I Were Pope

If I were pope
I'd proclaim the end of my infallibility
and banish the word sin from the doctrines of faith

I'd ask half the bishops and cardinals
to replace themselves with a thoughtful woman
and complete their ministries in a prison or homeless shelter

If I were pope
I'd pay the mystics to write poetry all day
and have their words read at the Sunday Masses

I'd pay the prophets to upload their message
in five minute videos
for youtube viewers around the world

I'd hire a thousand displaced workers
to construct a new Sistine Chapel and cover it with mirrors
instead of male images

If I were pope
I'd announce a contest
for 10 new sacraments that celebrate
peace-making, justice, and interfaith creations.

I'd send envoys to the villages
to talk about birth control
and distribute condoms wherever they are needed.

I'd establish a tuition-free college in every country
to train young students how to think
non-violently and act ethically.

If I were pope I'd convert closed churches
to housing for the needy
and meeting places for the marginal and walking wounded
I'd buy farms in rural places
and dedicate each one to organic farming
and cooperative, sustainable, community-based agriculture.

I'd convert every old Motherhouse and seminary
into a training center for spiritual activists, cultural creators
and community collaborators.

I'd auction off my skullcap, my mozetta cape and my darling red shoes
to the highest bidder and send the money to Haiti
for the construction of schools and health care centers.

I'd sell my Fisherman's Ring on ebay
and donate the proceeds to the Gulf shrimpers.

I'd trade my red and gold embroidered fascia
(the stole with the fringes) for a villa in Tuscany
and give free spa retreats to women who've served the church
for five years or more.

If I were pope, I'd throw a party at the Vatican
and invite everyone who's left the church
because they didn't feel welcomed.
(The overflow crowd would be treated to weekends
at Italian vineyards.)

If I were pope, I'd announce my retirement,
and as my last act in office, at the final party,
I'd ordain to the priesthood any woman who was ready,
marry any gay couple who wanted my blessing,
and marry any priest, male or female.

Then I'd get in my jammies,
say a prayer of gratitude,
and crawl into bed for a much needed nap.

COMPLINE (9:00 P.M.)

I am steeped in joy to be with you
yet I yearn to touch your face
Invisible One, I adore you
I adore everything you have made.

Here's some evidence of our evolving spiritual intelligence. I received an email today about a national conference where prominent progressive Christian theologians met with Christian Emergent leaders in what is purportedly the first such national event. According to one of the organizers, the conference was inspired by the current declining state of organized religion in America. What stood out to me was the format they followed.

The conference used an unusual process method, in which keynoters spoke for 12 minutes, followed by eight minutes of response from other event presenters, followed by another 20 minutes or so of questions that emerged after conversation between members of the audience.

This signifies a willingness to shift the ways we share information and elicit information from others. The model here is more engaged, more personal, more respectful of the intelligence and experience of each member in the room. It is evolu- tionary in that it taps the wisdom of the crowd. It operates from an awareness that the solutions will come from the multitudes interacting, not a singular entity dominating. The patriarchal structure may be giving way to a more feminine, receptive, organic form—a re-pairing of the opposites, a truly inspiring stride forward.

And I learned also from that email that Emergent Christian meetup groups are going on all across the country. People are sitting together in pubs, living rooms and church basements to midwife an emergent religion that has social and spiritual relevance, rituals of consequence and beauty, balance of powers. Oh, what a day!

Are you participating in church services that are lifeless and deadening to the imagination? Can you identify the problem? Can you do anything about it?

169

I woke up last night to the sound of laughing and realized I'd fallen asleep with the TV on. It was 3 AM and I knew it was Jon Stewart but I had to fumble around for my glasses to see who his guest was. Unbelievable! It was Jesus, in his robe and all. His nose was bigger than I thought, his skin a lot darker, but his eyes were more piercing than I'd ever imagined. It was like light came out instead of going into them.

Jon was making some joke about both of them being Jews and Jesus, after laughing harder than I thought he would, said quite seriously to Jon, "Yeah, that's one of the weirdest things, isn't it? How could they forget that?"

Jon was all over him with questions from the daily news. What was his take on the whole Mosque/Ground Zero fiasco? Jesus said he'd seen some newscasts on the story and couldn't believe the drama and fear it was bringing up. "They want to build a public building for prayer, education and community gathering. That's a good thing. A better thing perhaps, would be the construction of an interfaith building, There's room for everyone, and it's these distinctions between religions that's causing all the problems in the first place."

Jon looked incredulous. "An interfaith building??"

"Yes, a multi-tasking mosque, with a synagogue, chapel and meditation hall in it. A building where people of different faiths come together to make a better world together. That's the point of religion right? It's not about doctrine. It's a plan for action, an opportunity to be a communal force for good. Religion is just the map. Faith is the real adventure."

"I don't know...." said Stewart, making one of those funny mouth movements he does after hearing a strange idea.

Jesus pipes in, "What could be better in that spot than a building that represents, by its very structure, a coming together, a new vision that goes beyond religious borders? It's like taking a good idea and making it great. The real prophets of the day know this. Where are their voices? Why aren't you interviewing them?"

"Hmm, I thought I was," says Stewart, tapping his pencil on the desk.

"You know why you have border issues here? Because you believe the borders are real, like they MEAN something. Muslin against Christian, Mexican against American, Republican against Democrat—all those borders are made up. You put up walls to defend your ideas—and not even your OWN, but ideas passed down to you from someone else—and then you make other people look like demons. It's no wonder this country is falling apart. You don't even see how connected you are. You're like five fingers on a hand who think they're separate and make up reasons why not to get along."

Jon sat there with his mouth open.

"You're like children playing war games. You spend all your time attacking the "other side" instead of building a bridge to get across to a higher level of thinking. Even news shows are at war. Look at how you make fun of FOX. What light does that add to the world? All the time you could be giving to real visionaries, all the ways you could be role-modeling good behavior, showing the audience how it really WORKS to bring great and opposing minds together, and you sit there poking fun at another station. That's really enlightened, isn't it?"

This was the first time I'd ever seen Jon Stewart speechless. He looked like an embarrassed 6th grader. No pencil tapping now. More like a puppy with his tail between his legs.

"What in the world are you people doing? The ones who call themselves "religious" are often the most immature, the most judgmental and intolerant. What is THAT about? That's exactly the opposite of what every religion teaches. And I mean EVERY religion," Jesus said, as he looked away from Stewart and spoke right to the camera.

"All the religions say two basic things," he said, holding up his fingers in a peace sign. "First, there is no distance between you and this one you call God. God is the creative force behind all things. It's invisible, but you are the manifestation of it. I'm telling you, the Sistine Chapel should have been a mirror."

The audience laughs, but Stewart stares into the deep eyes of the Nazarene.

He goes on, " You are the eyes, the hands, the feet of that creative force. That energy is in you. It's called your breath." He holds up his index finger and taps on it a few times. "That's the first thing. Don't think there's some man out there pulling strings. Grow up. This civilization—if you can call it that—is YOUR creation. This earth, it is not a bunch of resources to be exploited. It is not to be owned. It is your mother, the womb that you sprang from. You are its consciousness, its neural cells. The whole earth is the organism that you belong to. You did not come down to earth, you came up from earth, as I did. Its well-being is in your hands. Can you be proud of what you're doing? Are you going to be the ones who kill it off, after all that talk about pro-life?"

Jesus was getting a little worked up, like that day he stormed through the temple turning over the merchants' tables. Jon cut to a commercial, "And we'll be right back to hear the 2nd basic thing from our guest tonight, ladies and gentlemen, the Jewish prophet Jesus of Nazareth. Stay tuned..."

They were laughing about something when they returned from the commercial, Jesus stretched out in his chair with his long lanky legs covered by his tunic, his sandaled feet hidden under the desk.

"OK," Jon says, "You were saying there were two things. Let me see if I got this right. There's no bearded guy up there on a cloud. That God we talk about and fight over is the creative force inside us and around us? It's invisible and we're like....(a long pause) its shadow?"

"Not exactly," says Jesus. We're like the physical form of the same energy. The ice cube version of water or steam. Same elements, different form. The sea and the iceberg. You're all icebergs in the Sea of God," he said, half-laughing at his own quaint metaphor. "But the problem is you don't realize that underneath it all, you're all connected. There's just one big iceberg with a lot of tips. The truth is, you're Creation continuing the co-creation of Itself."

"Oh my," says Stewart. "Let's leave that discussion to Bill Moyers, What about number two? What's the number two thing we're supposed to know?"

Jesus holds up his two fingers again, tapping the tip of his middle finger. The camera zoomed in so closely on him I could see a scar on his forehead. "It's not so much what you need to know—that's part of the problem, all these peoples' belief systems. That's what gets you in trouble. No one has to believe in me to get to heaven. A...there is no heaven to get to and B, it's not what you believe but how you act that matters. If anyone learned anything from reading that Bible they should have picked up that one. There's 3000 references to helping the poor in there. But let me get back..."

"Yes," says Stewart. "The second thing..."

"The second thing is this: forget everything you ever learned in any holy book and just treat everyone like a brother and a sister. I mean that literally. If it were your brother coming across the border...your sister with cancer and no health care....your child unable to get an education....your mother with no food in her house. And even further, your brother who was gay or hated gays, your sister who was a corrupt politician, your brother who bombed an abortion clinic, your sister who got an abortion. What does it look like to love unconditionally? To bridge differences, to come together over what we can agree on? Can you get through one day without thinking you're better or less than another? That's the thing to strive for. That is living faithfully."

"But...but..." says Stewart. "What about the Tea Partyers, the terrorists, what about Fox News and hate crimes?"

"If you think they are so different from you, be the opposite of what you think they are and enact that powerfully in the world. Don't focus on who's wrong. Just be a greater force for good."

"Not focus on who's wrong? How could I do my show?"

"Exactly. Remember what Gandhi said? Be the change you want to see in the world?"

"Sure. I have that quotation on my refrigerator."

"Well, it's time to take it further. You're evolving as a people. You've come through the Dark Ages, the Middle Ages, the Renaissance, the wrongly named Period of Enlightenment. You're now in the Information Age. You are growing your consciousness. In the physical world, you have Olympic marathon trainers who run 10 miles or more a day. They spend every waking hour in training, eating the right foods, researching the right clothing and equipment, working out, following a discipline. And in the metaphysical world, the spiritual world, you have people doing the same—they are your mystics and prophets—engaging in spiritual practice, accelerating their wisdom, expanding their consciousness, transcending judgment and radiating love into the world. You might be in that category."

Stewart does one of his choking, ahem things, putting his hand over his mouth. "Out of the question," he says frankly. "I thrive on judgment."

"Good to know yourself. You're all evolving at different rates. In the fall, when you look at a maple tree, you see leaves that are green, yellow, orange and red. They don't all change at the same time. And that's what makes life exciting. You all know different things. That's why you need each other. Like that guy Ken Wilber said, "You're all right, only partly so.""

Stewart nods his head in agreement, tapping his pencil on the table again.

"But back to Gandhi. I agree with what he said, but I'll say it a different way, just to shake things up a bit, which I love to do. By the way, it'd make a great bumper sticker: "Be the God you want to see in the world.""

"Oh-oh, sounds blasphemous to me," says Stewart.

"You know as well as I do, every good idea starts out as a blasphemy."

"OK, great, we're out of time," says Stewart, as the camera swings over for a shot of the audience. They're all standing, some crying and laughing at the same time, the most incredible look of collective awe I've ever seen. And Jesus walks over like Jay Leno and starts shaking hands with them. What a night!

*Mysticism is not about human abandonment into the arms of the divine,
but about immersion in the divine mystery at the heart of creation.*

Diarmuid O'Murchu (1947—)

MYSTICISM AND ONENESS

A woman sat in my workshop and waited for her turn to introduce herself and share why she had joined the ten week Conscious Creativity group. She was Irish, beautiful, red-headed and fair-skinned. "My name is Patricia," she said, "and I'm here because I want to be a mystic." We all had a good laugh, because it was such a novel idea, but the truth is, her goal was attainable. *Mystic* is one of those words that takes the imagination back a few centuries, conjuring up long religious habits, dark hallways, crucifixes, tears and holy stigmata. But put simply, a mystic is a person who has an unmediated experience of the Divine, whose sense of union with the Infinite is rooted in intuition and relationship more than beliefs and religion.

A mystic does not strive to find God. A mystic dwells in the Oneness that God is. Mystics do not experience separation anxiety. While there's always a yearning for what can't be seen, deeper than that is a wonder that seeing is not required. We don't need to see the wind to feel its force. Mystics experience a joy that can contain the world's sorrows. They are comfortable with paradox, in awe at life's complexities, dedicated to wholeness and the end of dualism. A mystic is one who draws attention to the unity and sacredness of what is, while a prophet is one who speaks out when that unity is disrupted. Like yin and yang, they are two aspects of one whole—the inner and the outer, the stillness and the action, the silence and the song.

Henri Bergson, in *The Two Sources of Morality and Religion*, writes of humanity laboring under the weight of its own inventions. It is as if we have grown too far ahead of ourselves, added to the body but not the soul, so that the extension of our physical capabilities is out of proportion to the refinement of our spirit. "Now, in this excessively enlarged body," he writes, "the spirit remains what it was, too small now to fill it, too feeble to direct it . . . Let us add that this increased body awaits a supplement of the soul and that the mechanism demands a mysticism."

Mysticism is demanded because we are poised on a perilous edge, at the brink where our choices will determine not what the future will bring, but whether there will *be* a future. Mysticism implies a heightened awareness of our oneness with the planet, the cosmos, the creatures and Creator. Without this consciousness of connectedness guiding and grounding us, the chances increase that we will abuse the technology we have so brilliantly conceived and constructed.

The same force that moves the planets, unfolds the petals of a rosebud, surges through a bolt of lighting, runs through us. Consciousness is embedded in all creation. When humankind became aware that it was aware, when we evolved to homo sapiens sapiens status—*the ones who know that they know*—the eyes of our planet opened up and the neural cells of her brain awakened. We were the earth feeling awe, nature adoring nature, infants looking into the face of the mother and knowing love for the first time.

As we grow in this awareness, becoming more intimate with ourselves, with the earth, with each other, our capacity to see and feel and heal expands. We intuit what is needed and respond. We see what is missing and offer that. We feel where there is pain, and place our hands upon it. We listen each other into being, offering ourselves in relationship, in service and joy. And our interactions then become more meaningful, heartening, wholesome.

If you wonder how to find passion in your life, look to see where you are needed, and go there full of fire and livingkindness. The Kingdom is all around us—in the turtles and tulips, the redwoods and rednecks. Wherever we look, there is the Divine. And until we *get* that, we will not reach out and create the relationships that will heal our wounds, repair our brokenness, and help us safeguard this earth, our mother.

MATINS (MIDNIGHT)

Though we're one, we seem to be many
Six billion and more is our count
yet sixty trillion cells in my body
equal one human being, not more.

One of the reasons why the traditional Judeo-Christian creation story is being updated is because it has God doing all the work before his rest on the seventh day. That story worked for awhile, but we have evolved beyond it now, having come to a point in history where humanity shares in the responsibility for which species survive and which do not. *We've got the whole world in our hands.*

As cultural historian Thomas Berry writes, "We live not simply in a cosmos but in a cosmogenesis." Things are still *unfolding*, and now we must face the fact that we are co-creators with huge decisions to make and extraordinary responsibilities. This is a choice point. We think ahead, or we die. We stop putting profit before everything, or we die. We raise our global consciousness and our spiritual intelligence, or we die.

We're the evolutionary creators of a New Era. The Age of Enlightenment we already went through didn't take. From all the news reports, one would think we were undergoing evolution in reverse. People still think life is happening *to* them, rather than *through* them. Preachers are still preaching the need for redemption. The only thing we need to be saved from is ourselves and our dangerous attachment to childish ideas. We're like a nation of teenagers who won't grow up.

Talking about "us" and "them" like our lives aren't intertwined is archaic. Thinking your own religion or party or nation has all the right answers is foolhardy and arrogant. Not admitting that you are co-creating the culture you live in is irresponsible. Our problems are rooted in the notion of separateness, while our solutions are suspended in the field of unity. Getting from here to there is a spiritual journey. Creating peace in our time is a spiritual undertaking because it involves imagination, hope, a vision of the future, a commitment to change. We can't call it in and wait for delivery. We have work to do, habits to change, neural networks to rewire. And *equally* important is the requirement to transcend duality, get beyond judgment, come to terms with our need for diversity, and our need as a people to value each other. This is the meaning and the mandate of spiritual intelligence.

Spiritually intelligent people can identify the distinctions between spirituality and religion. They know what it means to be "spiritual, but not religious" and they can be fully in relationship with people who are spiritual *and* religious or neither spiritual *nor* religious. The more diversity there is at the table, the more experience there is to draw from, and the more vital is the group's creativity. I have people in my family who are religious, but not spiritual. They say things like, "Let's go to Mass early and get it over with." They are not interested in talking about faith as a commitment to something here and now, faith as a propellant to compassionate action, faith as a guide to the choices we make all day long.

I think of it this way: religion is the menu, spirituality is the meal; religion is the score, spirituality is the music; religion is the poem, spirituality is its power. Mystics do not need religion to find God. They never lost God. They're not looking for their glasses, they're wearing them. To be one with the Divine takes attention and focus, commitment and practice. It's a state of awareness. It's personal, intimate, nobody's business.

If one doesn't aspire to mysticism, or to the Divine, it makes no difference. If one's faith is rooted in her/his ultimate concerns, grounded in the planet and disinterested in any heavens, it makes no difference. What we have in common is the realness of our lives, the urgency of these times, the callings of our soul to be a force for good. Spiritually intelligent people know this and they act on it. You can tell what they believe in from the living of their lives.

Ten years ago, astronomers told us there were 2 galaxies for every person alive. Now we know there's at least 18 for each of us. What changed?

Whoever does not see God in every place does not see God in any place.
Rabbi Elimelech

If God could talk
it wouldn't be in English
or Latin or Arabic
It wouldn't be in Yiddish
or Spanglish or pidgin

If God could talk
the words would crack like thunder
pour down like a torrent of jewels
flooding our basements with shining ideas,
sparkling conclusions.

If God could talk
a thought would be a redwood
a word an ocean
a sentence a century.

If God could talk
I would not have to
for all the words today requires
would flow in on the morning breeze
and find their way to the morning news.

If God could talk
God's word would be carried
on the wings of eagles
the ankles of gnats
in the pouches of kangaroos
and the paws of polar bears.

It would spread
through the sound of honey bees and hyenas
be translated into a rainbow
by blue herons and cardinals,
blackbirds and yellowjackets
pink flamingos and gray whales,
purple martins and chameleons.

It would cause rivers to flow,
tides to rise, moons to wax,
suns to set, sparrows to fly,
planets to revolve,
universes to expand
if God could talk.

LAUDS (SUNRISE)

The imperfection of the lower
is the invitation to the higher.
Chaos is humming
a love song to Order.

I pulled my car into the breakdown lane and grabbed my video camera. There was a flock of birds above Highway 194 that I couldn't keep my eyes off. There were hundreds of them performing a sky ballet that took my breath away. When I first looked, they were all white. Then they swooped down en masse, rolled over, and suddenly turned silver. When I looked again, they flew off in a new direction, and this time they all looked black.

Leaning up against my car hood, I turned on the camera and zoomed in on the flock. I had just focused in when I heard the sound of metal crashing into metal. Then everything became silent. I had one brief image of three things: my camera, my car, and myself flying through the air. Then everything went black.

When I came to, I was underneath my car, lying prostrate and facing the rear wheel. I lifted my head enough to see my outstretched arms and feared immediately that I was paralyzed. I tried to wiggle my fingers and was amazed when they moved. Then I tried my feet and my toes. They moved too. "I can get out of here," I thought. "I just have to shimmy out."

I tried to drag my body forward, but I couldn't move it. I was under the exhaust system, pinned to the ground, and the muffler was burning away my flesh. Now I realized I had to dig my way out. But it was high desert land, and with all my might, I could hardly make a scratch in the dry, hard dirt.

It was then I realized I was about to witness my own death. A great sorrow filled me at first when I thought of my mother having to hear I was killed in a terrible accident. Next came the assessment of how I had done with the life I was given. Did I have regrets? No. Was anything unfinished, unforgiven? No. Was I proud of the wake I left behind? Had I given all my thanks to everyone I was grateful for? "Yes," I thought. "I did the best I could do. If there's anyone to report to, I'll be proud to report."

It was time then to let go, but how could I do this? I wanted to live. I started to fear, not so much the unknown, but the end of the known. Then I thought of what I'd heard about the Native American elders who went to the mountaintop when their time had come. And I thought of the Inuit who went off to lie in a drift of snow when they knew the transition was close at hand. "I can do this," I thought. "If they could do it, I can do it." And I closed my eyes, took one last deep conscious breath, and began to slip backward, into the silence. I felt myself leaving through the soles of my feet, and was almost out when I heard the shouts.

"Is anybody there? Is anybody alive?" I zipped right back into my body and suddenly I was back under the car again. The frantic voices continued to call, "Is there anybody there? Is anyone alive?"

"I'm here," I called back, in a voice barely audible. "I'm alive."

I heard the sound of running feet. "Where are you?"

"Under the car, by the back tire."

I looked up and saw their legs. Two men. "Oh my God!" they cried out. "Wait there! We'll go get help!"

"Don't go," I pleaded. "You *are* the help. Just lift up the car."

There was a terrible silence, then they yelled back,

"We can't! We need help!"

"Yes you can," I cried. "You can. You're the help. Just lift it up...now."

And in one miraculous moment, they became the gods we are capable of being. They put their hands under the fender, and on the count of three, lifted the car as if it were an eagle's feather. Then two hands reached down to pull me out. They belonged to the man who had hit my car going seventy miles per hour.

I never knew it like I know it now—that *we* are the help and we need reminding.

When those men approached the wreckage, the first thing they experienced was their helplessness. They did not believe in their own powers and wanted to run off in search of help. They were caught in the story we've been told all our lives—that help is somewhere else, power and strength are somewhere else, the solutions are somewhere else, beyond us, outside of us. But when they heard that voice, *"You are the help,"* some shift happened. In the place of doubt rushed a huge and mighty force, a new belief that rippled through every cell in their bodies and infused their beings with whatever strength was called for.

Whatever is needed at this time in history to right this world, to right our own personal and precious lives, we have these things *within* us. We do not need science and technology to save us. We do not need government and religion to save us. We do not need more information and faster computers to save us. What we need is to abandon our notions that solutions exist somewhere else.

Coming to grips with the power we are is a necessary step on the evolutionary journey. It means being the ones we came here to be, believing in the words of the Master Teacher, *"Anything I have done in the name of the Creator, you can do, too...and even more."*

Mind does not exist in the plural and Mind is not separate from matter.

Erwin Schrödinger, physicist

Mysticism is an experience of communion. It is an embodied awareness of oneness, an intuitive recognition that the whole is in all of the parts. If religion were intelligence, mysticism would be wisdom. Mysticism is the outer brought inward. It is not the knowledge of something, but the experience of something. It is time to journey as far inwardly as we have journeyed outwardly, to rebalance ourselves by supplementing our souls as we have supplemented our bodies. Time to widen the highway between the brain and the heart.

Exit Interview

What was your work?
How did you help?
Where did you fail?
Who did you run to?
How did they help?
Who stood beside you?
What kept you going?
What seeds did you sow?
How did they grow?
What made you laugh?
What made you cry?
Who did they say you were?

How to Be a Mystic

Wake up every morning with thank you on your lips.

Brush your teeth with gratitude bubbling up in your mouth.

Leave the newspaper folded, the answering machine on and the door to your prayer place closed to the world till you have taken the call from the One Who Speaks in Silence.

Let your mind empty and fill with ten thousand thoughts and remember there is nothing that is not holy.

Be aware that the words you speak on Monday become the life you live on Thursday.

Look deeply enough into the eyes of those who speak to you that you see yourself in there.

Embrace thoughts that are contrary to yours and travel to the place where there is nothing to defend.

Crawl into bed at the end of the day singing thank you and thank you a hundred times.

If, as the result of some interior revolution, I were to lose in succession my faith in Christ, my faith in a personal God, and my faith in spirit, I feel that I should continue to believe invincibly in the world. The world (its value, its infallibility and its goodness) that, which when all is said and one, is the first, the last, the only thing in which I believe. It is by this faith that I live. And it is to this faith, I feel, that at the moment of death, rising above all doubts, I shall surrender myself. Teilhard de Chardin

We've Got the Whole World In Our Hands.

It is what it is
because that is what we are shaping,
what we are making of the clay in our hands.

There is no Gepetto pulling strings
causing gunfire, hurricanes, hunger
No god in some faraway sky blessing this one,
cursing the other
How long will you keep
placing your power on another's altar?

THIS is blasphemy:
that you regard the ordained as sacrament-makers
and go from street to street praying
someone else will come to feed the hungry.

The one who comprehends the truth of nothing to be attained is already seated in the sanctuary where he will gain his enlightenment. Huang Po

Christian civilization has proved hollow to a terrifying degree...Too few people have experienced the divine image as the innermost possession of their own souls. C.G. Jung

If there were classified ads for mystics and prophets, which job would appeal to you more? What job responsibilities would a mystic have that a prophet wouldn't, or vice versa? Can you see how these times are calling for us to be both? Mystics are needed to share the many ways of being in relationship with the Great Mystery without necessarily relying on a church or a clergy person. They are the ones whose first language is unity.

Prophets are needed to speak out when that unity is compromised or undermined by outside forces. It was a luxury of former times to choose one or the other. The requirement of this hour is to practice both: to steep ourselves in the wisdom of Deep Stillness and the knowing of Perfect Oneness, then to go out and stand firm against the forces that divide us.

Awe

The North Star is 5200 times brighter than our sun.
Light that enters my eyes has been traveling through space
at 186,000 miles per second every day for 316 years—
so fast it could have circled the earth
7 times in one second.

The light I see left the North Star
only 40 years after my ancestors landed at Plymouth
It takes light 130,000 years to go from one side
to the other of the Milky Way,
a small metropolis of 100 billion suns.

There are 100 billion galaxies in the universe
Light from the farthest one traveled
for 10 billion years before
the Hubble telescope snapped its photograph.

Now I lay me down to sleep.

Exploitation of the poor is to us a misdemeanor. To God it is a disaster.
Rabbi Abraham Heschel

If they watched you for a week, what would they say you value? Is that what YOU think you value?

Prime (6:00 a.m.)

Through my eyes you look out at your masterpiece
through my ears do you hear angels sing
through my hands do you heal the wounded
through my mouth do your words come to life.

Lillian Smith was born before women had the right to vote. A Southerner, she wrote to change southern society, to advocate for civil rights, to improve the cultural intelligence of her community and country. These are her words, from an era when "he" also meant "she" and "man" also meant "woman." I did not correct this. It is from her book, *The Journey:*

> Art, as is true of all man's profound experiences, is not for art's sake, nor for religion's sake, nor for the sake of beauty nor for any 'cause.' Art is for man's sake. The artist creates what he creates for himself as a living part of mankind…because of a passionate need to bring forth the inviolate part of his deepest experience and fuse it with elements of both earth and human past until it suddenly has a life of its own.

> And when he does this, other men call it theirs, also. The dialogue may rise and fall in cadence, now becoming a mighty chorus, in which the whole world seems to be participating, now only a whisper. But it never ceases. A time will come when it seems to rise again from the dead: that piece of sculpture, or an entire age of painting, or a book or poem—and once more, millions of men are talking with it, sharing their unborn dream with this ancient thing and taking from it what their dream needs to bring it alive.

> And by the listening and the sharing we not only are enriched but we bestow wealth on our world. For we are "in dialogue," we are forming a new quality of human relationship. In doing so, we are, as Henry Miller has said, "underwriting our age with our lives," because we believe utterly in its power to transmute its terror and grief and sorrow and mistakes into a music which the future can claim as its

own. And yet, how alone the artist feels in his ordeal…

But the artist is never alone. He has an intimate relationship with the wood he is carving, the paint and canvas, the words, the stone: these are making their demands and their plea and offering their gifts and he is answering and the dialogue sustains him—as do another man's beliefs and memories and the knowledge that there are those who care.

The artist knows something else, wordless, oftentimes, but he knows it deep within him: that were it not for the struggle and the loneliness he undergoes in his search for integrity there would be no strength or beauty in his work. And though art is not for the sake of beauty, *beauty must be there or the profound revelation the artist makes would be unbearable.* (italics mine)

The artist in us knows, the poet in us knows: *it is the mark not of ordeal but of mastered ordeal that gives a face, a life, a great event, or a great work of art its style. The wound is there, but the triumph also,* the death and the birth, the pain and the deep satisfactions: it is all there in delicate equilibrium, speaking to us.

Have you mastered all of your ordeals?

Hope is the energy that sustains a new vision while it transforms from the realm of the imagination into the realm of manifest reality. Hope is the child of longing and expectation. It is desire in love with wisdom. Prayer married to thanksgiving. Hope is not a powerless waiting for, but a powerful welcoming of the future we are creating. It is an evolutionary act that totally engages the body, mind and spirit. Hope is not business as usual. It is re-orienting to a new star.

What is it you're hoping for?

TERCE (9:00 A.M.)

My skin is an interesting boundary
like a pail of water at sea
within me, you slosh and churn
outside you're the ocean to me.

I was teaching a classed called Marry Your Muse at the International Women's Writing Guild Summer Conference. It was my first opportunity to be with writers exclusively, and I was surprised when they all started sharing their reasons for *not* writing. For some it was not enough time, not the proper space to write in, no support from their spouses, too many demands from children and partners; but for others the obstacles were buried deeper: I don't believe I have a story worth telling, no one is interested in what I have to say, it's too hard to deal with all the rejection.

I learned that morning that the class wasn't about becoming a better writer, but clarifying the importance of writing itself. It was not a How-To, but a Why-To. We spent the week writing our way right through the barriers—saying out loud what they were, engaging with them creatively to get some sparks flying, imagining there was some reason they once showed up, thanking them for that and letting them go. We burrowed in deeply to find our Muse, to discover our voice and practice releasing it into the world. We shared our words with each other and felt together the feelings they drew to the surface.

By the end of the week, we had an intimate relationship with the Voice Within and planned a wedding ceremony with our Muses for the last day of class. Each woman wrote her vows to the Muse addressing the obstacle she was there to break through. Each vow became a reframe of the thing that had held her back. They had taken their lanterns to the darkest places, encountered the shadow, and returned with the wisdom that dark had to offer. There was no fear anymore, less hesitation, resolute conviction to their creative spirits as they proclaimed their vows on this holy day.

The whole event lingered with me for days—the hope of it, the joy of it, the memories of our circle and the elegance of their vows. I didn't want anyone to forget, so I wrote the Artist's Creed and sent it out to each of them as a constant reminder: *This is what we agreed on; this is what we committed to. Never forget that your words are food to the hungry soul.* And this creed became the seed for the book *Marry Your Muse*, which takes each tenet and fleshes it out. This is how it works. This is how we make the world anew through the creations of our lives.

The Artist's Creed

I believe I am worth the time it takes to create
whatever I feel called to create.

I believe my work is worthy of its own space
which is worthy of the name sacred.

I believe that when I enter this space, I have the right
to work in silence, uninterrupted, for as long as I choose.

I believe that the moment I open myself to the gifts of the Muse,
I open myself to the Source of All Creation, and become
one with the Mother of Life Itself.

I believe that my work is joyful, useful, and constantly changing,
flowing through me like a river with no beginning and no end.

I believe that what it is I am called to do
will make itself known when I have made myself ready.

I believe that the time I spend creating my art
is as precious as the time I spend giving to others.

I believe that what truly matters in the making of art is not what the
final piece looks like or sounds like, not what it is worth or not worth,
but what newness gets added to the universe in the process
of the piece itself becoming.

I believe that I am not alone in my attempts to create,
and that once I begin the work, settle into the strangeness,
the words will take shape, the form find life, and the spirit take flight.

I believe that as the Spirit gives to me, so does she deserve
from me: faith, mindfulness, and enduring commitment.

Think of someone's creation that has changed your life: a novel you've read, a song you love, a movie or play you've seen. Imagine your own words and stories lingering in the lives of others, comforting or guiding, inspiring or enlightening. What are you waiting for to be of use? What holds you back from sharing yourself?

When I was a child, eleven or twelve
I'd pray to be a martyr every night.
"Please, God, let me die for you"
I'd beg from my knees at the side of my bed
in training to be a soldier of Christ.

I think of that when I read
of the young suicide bomber,
his parents proud,
his body exploded into bits

My prayers changed when I learned
the difference between faith and religion
and chose the one that lifted me up.
What I believe in thins out to transparency
more often than not.
No words can describe
the Nothingness I belong to,
and the joy it brings me.

Think about it: Happiness in the US peaked in 1956. I was seven. Now we have the highest average income, the greatest income inequality, and 58% of us will spend at least one year below the poverty line. How is this related to spiritual intelligence?

Borderless Prince

I know he's here
I'm breathing anyway
No need for other signs
or recordable evidence-no need to
thrust my hand into some bloodied wound
We're in a new world now
and all I'm hoping for is an opposite
to fuse with
some spirit to my matter,
a touch of north to my south,
some yin to my yang.

I don't need a thundering force
setting bushes on fire
or a star in the east lighting up the desert sky.
I'm not asking for a miracle on a mountaintop.
All I want is a tango with the Other
a cheek to cheek with the Invisible One
a two step with the Eternal One

I want to merge and cry out and tumble about
in the arms of the Other
showering him with earth
as he blesses me with heaven

I want to hear that rumbling moan of quenched desire
The sound of union, real as flesh
The whoosh of dissolving borders, melting margins
The celestial choir belting out Hallelujah to the midnight sky
while comets weave webs with their tails of light.

Sext (Noon)

There are mystics who live on Broadway
mystics who live on Main
they are the ones who find You
though You hide again and again.

It's Jalene's turn to have fifteen minutes of our attention in our class on Evolutionary Creativity. She's in her mid-thirties, long dark hair, a lean healthy body, and a face as radiant as the sky at dawn. We're sitting in a horseshoe shape— 16 of us— and she lays out four Flamenco dresses on the floor in the center. Her hair is tied back in a bun, and she has on a red necklace, red earrings and a brilliant red comb in her hair. There's a flower in her ear, and she is wearing a Spanish flamenco tiered skirt. She hands me two CDs and asks me to play them when I get her cue.

Jalene shares with us about the first time she walked through her fear, boarded a plane for Spain, and spent a year there learning flamenco. She speaks for awhile of her personal journey, then begins the story of becoming pregnant and the joy it brought to her and her husband. She speaks of the attention they gave to the decision to get pregnant, and the many the ways she prepared herself through the months to come—the yoga, the massages, the foods she ate, the music she played, always with the hope the little one would like it. She searched throughout the city for two midwives she trusted and the day finally came for the child to be born.

Jalene's voice cracks here as she speaks of his death at the moment of birth— a tragedy that occurred only three months ago. His name was Elan Vie, from the Hebrew and French for the *tree of life*, the *passion of life*. As she stands there before us, she wraps her arms around herself and cries and cries. Tears are flying from her eyes. Those of us in our seats lean forward in rapt and focused compassion, witness to a mystery unfolding before us. Many of us cry right along with her, men and women both wiping tears from our eyes.

When the sorrow abates, she cues me for the music and begins to dance her evolutionary creative art piece. The music is traditional Sevillanas festive music, filled with light and joy. Jalene whirls her way around the group, stopping long enough in front of each of us to make a connection that is deep and dear. After two minutes of flamenco, the lights go down and the music changes to *Grace* by Snatam Kaur.

Jalene spreads her white shawl as an altar cloth on the floor, placing upon it a candle and a copper bowl. She fills the bowl with water from her bottle, bows down, and removes her earrings, necklace and the red comb from her hair. As she unpins her hair, long dark curls cascade down her back. Jalene bows again before the altar, blesses the water, and pours it over her head. The water splashes down her hair and shoulders, falling like teardrops into her lap and onto her skirt. The moment is sacred. Nobody moves. On her knees still, she bends over in sorrow, and begins to sob.

Her sorrow moves around us like a fog rolling in. Each of us feels her grief as we breathe in the air. The strings and piano offer their comfort. The walls and the windows watch in agony. When Jalene's sobs subside, we turn off the lights and sit still in the silence while her pain makes its way through our hearts.

I kneel next to Jalene and ask if she minds if we keen out our sorrow, a Gaelic tradition of vocal lament where women at the graveside moan and wail. Jalene nods and we turn the lights completely off. I lay down on the floor, with my head on my arms. Then I begin to wail and cry. Others follow and people move from their chairs down to the floor. The room is dark. The wailing is deep. The sound of our mourning cannot be described.

When the keening stops of its own accord, I lean over to wrap my arms around Jalene, and feel in the dark several hands already there, stroking her back, rubbing her shoulders and water-blessed head. Hardly a body is left in the seats, as we'd gravitated toward the center and the source of the pain. Our hands and arms intermingle as one as we reach out to comfort this childless mother. We were like cells in a body, coming to the aid of a part that is wounded. Moving in the dark, on our bellies and knees, we lean into the hurt one, reaching out in love.

When the sound dies down and the lights come up, the sight of us together is a vision in itself—sprawled out in a circle around the grieving mother, we are petals to the rose of her, channels for her tears. We stand up in silence, hold each other in wonder, and look long and deep into each other's teary eyes.

While we mourned the loss of a baby that night, we gave birth to something new—birth to an awareness of the power of ritual, and birth to a sacred circle that will never be the same.

Four days later, I attended Sunday services at the Unity Center where we meet for class. When I walked toward the sanctuary, I saw a huddle of people gathered in a circle. It was us! Still in awe, still whirling, still speechless...but in love with each other on the heels of that grace.

The following Wednesday when we met for class, I asked if anyone wanted to share how our experience had affected for them during the week. Roy said he had never seen anyone be so vulnerable in front of others before and it helped him feel less afraid about sharing his feelings. Allie, Jalene's mother, said the ritual contained all of the sacraments, from baptism to last rites, including her daughter's ordination as a high priestess, and that it felt like we were all one in the universal womb. Martha had never been in such uncharted territory before, and felt the whole ceremony was a communion service. Jennifer said it felt like Jalene went through the fire and came out a phoenix, and that she was a midwife to each of us doing the same. Katy sensed an expansion of oneness she'd never felt before. David felt as if we had all been banded in some holy way. Burt felt honored to reach that level of intimacy as a group.

It had been transformative for each of us, as sacred ceremonies are meant to be. And the reason is that every one of us was engaged in the moment, 100 percent present, driven only by an urge to heal and be a witness. We were co-celebrants in a sacrament of public grieving. The spontaneity of it was important, the fearlessness was important, the lights being out was important, the tenderness and wailing was important.

This is why there is no official rulebook for the celebration of rituals we're creating these days. The grace is in the movement of spirit, the creative combustion, the risk of being real, vulnerable and original. One has to be open. Spirit flies into open windows.

The only news I know
Is bulletins all day
From Immortality.
            Emily Dickinson

NONE (3:00 PM)

Your words and thoughts
are your yarn and knitting needles.
Your life is the afghan, the mittens, the scarf.
If you work with wool and cotton threads
you will never end up with a cashmere sweater.

Peter Tompkins and Christopher Bird offer fascinating accounts of the consciousness in matter in their book, *The Secret Life of Plants.* One experiment performed by a medical director and chemist involved a male subject who had brought a philodendron he had nursed from a seedling and cared for tenderly. The two scientists attached a polygraph to the plant and asked the owner a series of questions, instructing him to give false answers to some of them. The plant had no trouble indicating through the galvanometer which questions were answered falsely.

To see if a plant could display memory, six blindfolded polygraph students drew folded strips of paper from a hat. One of them contained instructions to root up, stamp on, and thoroughly destroy one of the two plants in a room. The criminal was to commit the crime in secret. No one knew his identity, and only the second plant would be a witness. When the surviving plant was attached to a polygraph, the students paraded before it one by one. The plant gave no reaction to five of them, but when the actual culprit approached, the meter went wild.

Even robots have been documented responding to the power of thought. Eighty different groups were tested in one experiment involving a robot and baby chicks. A robot was sent into a room full of baby chicks in bright daylight, and its movements were all observed to be random in nature. Knowing that the chicks prefer well-lit rooms, the researchers then devised an experiment where they turned off all the lights, leaving the chicks in the dark. They then sent in a robot carrying a lighted candle. In 71 percent of the cases, the robot spent excessive time in the vicinity of the chicks. Its former random movements were now affected by the desire of the chicks for its light. There is mind in all matter.

Physicist Max Planck wrote, "All matter originates and exists only by virtue of a force which brings the particles of an atom to vibration and holds this most minute solar system of the atom together....We must assume behind this force the existence of a conscious and intelligent mind. This mind is the matrix of all matter." The *who* that we are is one with this very matrix. We are the vessels through which it operates, as the light bulb is a vessel for electricity. The force comes through us, taking whatever shape we give it. Whether one is a terrorist or a piano tuner, a murderer or a mystic, the very same force is within each individual, holding the atoms and cells together, unifying us in the web of existence. As the poet Dylan Thomas put it,

> The force that through the green fuse drives the flower
> Drives my green age...

When Einstein reached the conclusion that "something deeply hidden had to be behind things," it is this force he was talking about. When the Indian mystic Sri Aurobindo wrote, "That within us which seeks to know and to progress is not in the mind but something behind it which makes use of it," he, too, was referring to the Great Consciousness of which we are a part and to whom we belong.

You don't discover God first, then live a compassionate life. The practice of disciplined sympathy would itself yield intimations of transcendence. Religious teaching is never a statement of objective fact: it is a program for action.

Karen Armstrong

Moishe has been looking for a parking place for twenty minutes.

Filled with despair he raises his eyes and says: "My God, if you get me a parking space in five minutes, I promise I'll eat kosher food for the rest of my life."

Then suddenly, right next to him, a car drives away leaving an ideal parking spot. He looks up again and says: "God, stop searching, I found one!"

VESPERS (SUNSET)

Though they say you live in the heavens
a billion miles away
O what delight to find you
in my room at the break of each day.

The issues of poverty, global warming, species extinction will never be solved by our talking, our coursework, our panels and commissions. They are emotional issues and solutions will never occur to us until we open our emotions and feel their impact—until we are struck by a grace that helps us see the real meaning behind *what you do for the least of them, you do for me.*

Evolutionary creators traverse constantly between the private and the public, deepening themselves in silence and study, then reaching out with what they've gained on the inner journey. Their energy, then, is whole and integral; their intelligence is embodied; and in their words and every action is a power that others identify as a force for good. It is this integration of inner and outer, self and other, insight and action that fuels the work of prophets and mystics.

Because everything we do and everything we are is in jeopardy, and because peril is immediate and unremitting, every person is the right person to act and every moment is the right moment to begin. Jonathan Schell

A conversation in the year 2050 between a boy and his grandfather:

Grandpa, did you know it was happening?
Well, sort of. There was news about it, but it didn't seem too real.

How did it feel when you couldn't eat the fish anymore?
Well that was hard. We never thought that would happen.

Didn't they warn you?
Not really. I guess some tried to, but not in a big way. Not like on television, or even much in the newspapers. You had to really want

to know, I guess. People just didn't care that much. We were pretty busy then. Pretty caught up in our own lives.

What about the forests? Didn't you know how much we needed them, just to breathe?
People never thought about that connection, son. We needed that timber. Companies needed it for their business. That's what was important back then. Business.

But why would you let them take away everything we needed? Why did you let them make all those stupid things out of plastic? Why didn't you save some of the oil for us?
I swear, we never thought we'd use it up. We weren't trained to think about the future. No one taught us how to think. We did the best we could do, day by day.

I thought you were smart. You had your own business, didn't you?
Yes.

If you were so smart, why didn't you stop them from ruining all the water? Didn't you ever think I might want to swim like you used to?
It's not like that.

Oh yes it is. If you were so smart you would have known what was happening. But you didn't care. It's your fault.
It's not my fault, son. There were millions of us here. Everyone was to blame.

Then why didn't they stop it? Why did they ruin things for us? Why didn't you care enough to *do* something? Why? Why? WHY?

One of the women in our Gnostic Gospel Choir started a Threshold Choir of women to sing at the bedside of the dying. They had only been meeting for a few weeks when Nadean, the director, got a call requesting the choir's services. Since the Threshold Choir was not yet ready, Nadean called upon us, a group of women who've been singing for eight years and who sang on my CD *Singing for the Soul*.

Could we come to sing at the bedside of a woman close to death? Several of us stopped what we were doing and went to the home of the woman's family, where she was lying in a hospital bed in the living room. We circled round her bed, next to her family and her hospice nurse, and sang along to our CD to bring her whatever comfort we could. Song after song, it dawned on each of us that every word we sang felt as if we had written it for that very occasion.

I will not leave you comfortless
I will not leave you alone
I am the air you breathe in
I'm the light of every star and every dawn.

Then there was the prayer chant *Come Be Beside Us, Come Be Around Us, Come Be Within Us, Come Be Among Us*, calling in the spirits who would usher her out and asking those who'd gone before her to be there at her side. We sang The Yoruba song *Yemaya Assessu*, about the river returning to the Sea, our beautiful *I and the Mother Are One*, *Holy Woman*, *I See Myself in You*, *My Body, My Temple*, and finally *I'll Fly Away*.

When we recorded those songs, none of us had an inkling we'd be singing them at a deathbed, and yet when the family acknowledged how meaningful it was to them, we said it felt like we'd been practicing for eight years for that very occasion.

The Creative Force is still exploding, expanding our universe in a thousand directions every moment. And so, too, is it exploding in us, turning into creations that bring comfort and joy. It is not always for us to know what exactly this force has in mind, but to be a vessel for its power, a humble servant of its grace and wonder. That family will never forget the tenderness of these strangers who walked into their home, stood beside their sister, circled like a tribe and sang her home with songs for her soul.

COMPLINE (9:00 P.M.)

Everything I'm not, You are
Everything I am, You are
This mind that beholds and addresses You
This is You. You speaking to you.

To live inspired, spiritually intelligent lives doesn't take genius, money, or luck. It takes time, the courage to go within, and the commitment to a daily practice of communion with the Infinite. It is this union that enables us to ignore the petty voices within and around us and preserve our magnitude amid waves of mediocrity. Just as our bodies need food and water to sustain them, our souls need solitude and silence. It's the medium of their expression. Without this, we have no means to hear their message.

Why scurry about looking for the truth? It vibrates in everything and every not-thing, right off the tip of your nose. Can you be still and see it in the mountain? The pine tree? Yourself? Don't imagine that you'll discover it by accumulating more knowledge. Knowledge creates doubt, and doubt makes you ravenous for more knowledge. You can't get full eating this way. Lao-tzu

We attract experiences supporting our deepest beliefs. What are your beliefs and what experiences are they attracting? What might you want to discard?

I was carpooling in an RV with two women from San Diego, heading for Santa Fe, New Mexico where I was leading a workshop. Halfway there, my artist friend Jane announces she's an atheist.

"Jane," I say, "You're going to a workshop called Divining the Body. You're going to be the only atheist in the room."

"That's ok. I usually am."

"What do you do when everybody talks about God like they do?"

"Oh, I'm used to it now. You can forget about it. It won't matter."

200

But I *couldn't* forget about it. I drove hundreds of miles pondering how I could make this feel as good for Jane at it was going to feel for everyone else. I didn't want her to feel excluded. I didn't want to use a language that was foreign to her. My job as a facilitator is to create a sense of oneness, and I had my work cut out for me, I could see that.

We stopped at the Albuquerque airport to pick up three women from Missouri who started talking about God the moment they arrived. God did this. God did that. Every time I hear the word, my ears burn. I wonder how it feels to have everyone talking as if they just got a text message from God himself when you have no belief whatsoever in an external Almighty Heavenly Father.

"It was raining, but God got us a great taxi-driver who got us there on time."

"I was married to an alcoholic, but God set it up that way so I'd learn patience.

"God helped me find just the right man on e-harmony…God gave me a child with disabilities…God gave me cancer because…"

Every time I heard the word God, I wanted to say "Who exactly are you talking about and how does this work?"

We pulled into the parking lot and had two hours before our first gathering. I still had no idea how to handle things, but a thought occurred to me as I entered our meeting room. We sat in a circle and I said to the group, "There's only one rule for the entire weekend. You can share anything you want, but you can't used the word 'God.'"

"Why not?"

"Because we're trying an experiment—we're trying to take things to a deeper level here, broaden our ways of understanding and expressing our relationship with the Source. If we have to come up with new ways to describe what we're talking about, we'll get clearer about what it really is…because we won't be able to fall back on a conceptual word that might not work for everyone in our presence. It's a global world now and we have to practice relating to people who don't necessarily share the same notion of God."

They agreed and we kept the rule all weekend, with just a few little slips. By Sunday lunchtime, an incredible energy surged through our group. Women were grounded in their speaking and their words radiated with self-authority. They claimed their wisdom, shared their journeys, and took full responsibility for the lives they had created. Though it didn't come naturally in the early stages, by the end of the weekend they were pros in communicating their essence. No one had to point to the heavens, abdicate their power, give credit to the Father. Instead they praised themselves, acknowledged their courage, and claimed the very gifts that the disciples of Jesus failed to claim—their ability to do whatever he had done.

This is how we're served by the ideas of "the other." The spirituality of each of us was deeply affected that weekend, and it wouldn't have happened if we hadn't had an atheist in our midst.

He is Cosmic Intelligence, Mind at Large
She is Wisdom, making soup and bread
from his stellar ideas.

He is night-time, twilight, dawn and daylight
She is the Serengeti, the rainforest,
Lover's Lane and Death Valley.

He is silence, stillness, a cavern of nothingness
She is birdsong, lovemaking, the laughter of children

He is the heat of the Sahara desert
She is the sand in the palm of his hand.

He is space all boundless and infinite
She, a galaxy wrapped in his arms.

He is the fire, She the volcano,
spewing new earth from his molten seed.

He is the sea, and She the wave,
He the wind, She the wheat fields

All day long they rise and roll
lean and bend, like teenagers
locked in love's embrace.

All life grows from the union of the two
When two become one, the New rises up.

Preparing for the Sacrament of Holy Unity

I will need around me a birch tree, a maple, a redwood, a white pine,
a sequoia, a cedar, a palm tree.

I want soil from Nigeria, Palestine, the Himalayas, Mississippi, Auschwitz,
Oklahoma City, Maui, Alcatraz.

I want water from the Mediterranean Sea, The Baltic, the Ganges River, Glacier
Bay, the Sea of Galilee, the Tigris and Euphrates, the Pacific and the Atlantic,
the River Jordan, the Dead Sea, Lake Bonaparte, Niagara Falls.

I want air from Kathmandu, Calcutta, Cairo, Nazareth, Athens, the Arctic Circle, Mexico City, Port-au-Prince, Baghdad, Kabul.

I want near me a bison, a wolf, an eagle, a silverback gorilla, a giraffe, a kitten,
a fawn, a black bear, a polar bear, a golden retriever.

From the waters, I want a humpback whale, a porpoise, a sea turtle, a manta
ray, a flounder, a harp seal.

From the heavens I want a comet, a rainbow, a lightning bolt, a blue moon, a
summer storm, a snowy night, a mauve and golden sunrise.

I want fire from my morning candle, the farthest star in the Milky Way, a campfire in the Adirondacks, the altar at St. Joseph's Provincial House, the funeral
pyres in Varanasi, the Buddhist temples in Kyoto.

I want a vestment made of materials from Gujarat, India; Lhasa, Tibet; Cape
Town, South Africa; St. John's, Newfoundland; Oslo, Norway; northern Ireland;
central Australia; East Germany; and South Central Los Angeles.

I want an altar made of rocks from Rajasthan, Alexandria, the Acropolis, Canyon de Chelly, the Grand Canyon, Vermont, Italy, Sedona, Syracuse and Sendai.

I want co-celebrants from an Ethiopian village, a Harlem tenement, a preschool in Pokhara, a nursing home in Selma, a prisoner in Guantanamo, a Harvard Law class, the Smokey Mountain garbage dump in Manila, the Mormon Tabernacle Choir.

I want bread kneaded and pressed by the hands of millionaires, chambermaids, sherpas, Bolivian tin workers, emigrants and immigrants from a hundred countries, three Fortune 500 CEOs, nine Exxon board members, 14 Chicago gang members, and seven out of work shrimpers from the Gulf of Mexico.

I want a choir of Chinese peasants, Israeli kindergartners, Japanese Bonsai masters, Navajo weavers, Zuni potters, Tlingit totem pole makers, and African diamond miners.

Once assembled, we will celebrate the sacrament that contains them all.
We will sing till the earth wobbles in her orbit,
give praise and thanks till wine runs from the sugar maple.

We will bow to the holiness we see in each other
forgiving the past, blessing the present,
committing to a future that is good for everyone.

And this will be the sacrament of Holy Unity
a welcome to the dawning of an Uncommon Era.

Book Club Guidelines for No Ordinary Time

1. Chapter One—Awakening

Jean Gebsen writes about the "agonies of emerging consciousness" in the book's introduction. Think of moments of awakening that you have experienced and share your stories, including the difficult aspects of letting go of the old.

Go around the circle and have each person identify a few beliefs they once held but no longer do. What caused you to change your mind?

The programming we inherit from our culture and religions runs wide and deep through our mental terrain. I once asked a Jewish businessman how he determined what issues to support? He said, "I ask three questions: Is it good for the Jews? Is it good for the poor? Is it good for the Blacks? And if it is, I support it." What values guide you in your moral decisions? How does your faith come into play?

How would your life change if you "gave each task all the time it requires?" If someone watched you for a week, what would they say you valued most?

The story of "Go First" suggests we can have the kind of meaningful conversations we want to have, but we have to initiate them. Is it difficult for you to start conversations that involve your feelings and values? If so, why do you think this is true?

2. Chapter Two—Discipline

Committing to a discipline is something that people have a hard time doing. Think of some things you do ritualistically and never even think about it. What makes it easy to commit to that? What makes it difficult to commit to twenty minutes of silence and solitude a day?

Go around the group and inquire how people are taking care of themselves in body, mind and spirit.

Reflect on the Zen student who asked how long enlightenment would take and the Master said ten years. When the student said "What about if I work twice as hard and double my effort?" the Master replied, "Twenty years." Deepak Chopra says "Effort is the problem, not the solution." What do you make of this?

Zen Master Sozan and Catholic priest Anthony de Mello both gave the same advice: Give up your opinions and you will see truth. What does this mean?

CHAPTER THREE: CREATIVITY AND THE NEW COSMOLOGY

Ask the question, "Do you feel that life is happening through you or to you?" Go around the room and see what surfaces.

Read aloud the quotation from Audre Lorde on visibility. Have people share a time when they transformed silence into language and felt some kind of shift or transformation.

The book identifies how to spot a false prophet. How do you recognize a true prophet?

Have the group come up with some names of a few contemporary prophets.

The book suggests that releasing our emotions is a way letting the Divine flow into the world. Have a conversation about why is it sometimes challenging to reveal our emotions.

Consider the value of the creations you've encountered—the plays, movies, novels, poems that have touched your life. Each of these was the result of the creator bringing the inside out. Go around the room and ask each person, "What exists in the world because you are alive. Besides children, what else have you created and brought to life?"

CHAPTER FOUR: THE MYSTERY OF EVIL

The book suggests we counter evil by bringing its exact opposite into the world. What does that mean and how does it look?

In her story about processing her dismissal from the convent, the author acknowledges at the end that there was nothing to forgive. Once she had a witness to her story and was truly heard, she no longer had to hold on to bitterness and rage. Have a conversation about getting to the place where there is nothing to forgive.

If you had the power to fix any problem or evil in the world, what area would you focus on? Can you do some small thing toward that happening in your life today?

The author says "If we cannot hear an opposing idea without having a negative reaction, we are not free." Do you agree with this?

Teilhard de Chardin said we are coming to a point where we have to choose between suicide and adoration. How does this feel? What causes you to be in awe or adoration?

Holocaust survivor Elie Wiesel says "Not to transmit an experience is to betray it." What do you think he means by that?

CHAPTER FIVE: NON-DUALITY

The philosopher/poet Beaudelaire said "The quality of true genius is the ability to hold two contradictory thoughts simultaneously without losing your mind." Practice this in the group. Take a thought that you believe in, then make a case for how its opposite is true.

How does it make you feel to be in the presence of someone who is entirely opposite from you? Can you accept that the more willing to are to unite with the "other," the more creative you will become?

What is it that makes non-dualistic thinking evolutionary?

What happens to you when you imagine the Sacred as Feminine?

CHAPTER SIX: JOY AND DESIRE

Reflect on the story of Sr. Bette Ann and the Pete Seeger concert. Did you ever have an impulse like that that was thwarted? What do you need to keep your dreams alive?

The author shares a story about her high school teacher introducing her to poetry that changed her life. How was your life altered by an adult influence? In what ways are you affecting the lives of today's youth?

The author talks about people having to leave their churches for a variety of reasons having to do with justice and integrity. Have people share their stories about their changing relationships to the churches they belong to or reasons why they left.

CHAPTER SEVEN: MYSTICISM AND ONENESS

Have the group define what a modern day mystic is. Does anyone come to mind that fits the bill? Is there a value to the human family in having mystics? What role do they play?

What are some of the qualities of spiritual intelligence? Do any public figures come to mind whom you consider spiritually intelligent? How are they contributing to our society? How are you contributing?

Read the Lillian Smith piece aloud and have a conversation about mastered ordeal and what it means.

The author speaks about praying to be a martyr. She equates her training with the training that young suicide bombers get. Does that ring true?

AUTHOR BIO

Jan Phillips is an evolutionary artist, author, workshop director and social activist. She is co-founder and Executive Director of the Livingkindness Foundation (www.livingkindness.org), a global network of grassroots philanthropists turning creativity into compassionate action. Jan is also co-founder of Syracuse Cultural Workers, publishers of artwork for social justice and global consciousness. (www.syracuseculturalworkers.com)

She has taught in 23 countries, made a peace pilgrimage around the world, produced 2 CDs of original music, and created several videos on the power of creativity to transform consciousness. Her other books include *The Art of Original Thinking-The Making of a Thought Leader, Divining the Body, Marry Your Muse, God is at Eye Level—Photography as a Healing Art, Making Peace, Born Gay,* and *A Waist is a Terrible Thing to Mind.*

As a performing artist/speaker, Jan brings music, poetry, and images to all her audiences, using the arts to inspire as well as inform. Blending east and west, art and activism, reflection and ritual, Jan's transformational presentations provoke original thinking and evolutionary action. With stories, humor and cutting edge creativity, she connects the dots between science, spirituality and social action. Visit www.janphillips.com for her books, CDs, videos and calendar of workshops.

No matter what our attempts to inform, it is our ability to inspire that will turn the tides. —from Marry Your Muse